Historical and Traditional Sketches of Highland Families and of The Highlands

John Maclean

HERITAGE BOOKS
2015

HERITAGE BOOKS

AN IMPRINT OF HERITAGE BOOKS, INC.

Books, CDs, and more—Worldwide

For our listing of thousands of titles see our website
at
www.HeritageBooks.com

A Facsimile Reprint
Published 2015 by
HERITAGE BOOKS, INC.
Publishing Division
5810 Ruatan Street
Berwyn Heights, Md. 20740

Originally printed in
Inverness, 1895
John Maclean

International Standard Book Numbers
Paperbound: 978-0-7884-0809-0
Clothbound: 978-0-7884-6175-0

PREFACE TO THE SECOND EDITION.

———o———

THE first edition of Maclean's Historical and Traditional Sketches appeared at Dingwall in 1848. The book has long been out of print, and copies appearing for sale have usually brought double the price at which the work was originally published, and a constant demand for copies has induced the present publisher to issue a second edition. While giving the original text *verbatim*, the editor has endeavoured by notes to correct statements as to families and individuals and to give additional information from reliable sources, and documents in his possession. The writer of these Sketches was Finlay Maclean, a son of the " Inverness Centenarian," and he undoubtedly obtained most of his stories from the rich source of the retentive memory of his father; but he was in the habit of adding from other channels matters that the Centenarian had not repeated, or had not the knowledge of. For many years he did penny-a-lining for several northern newspapers, and the present work shows in some cases his stories " long drawn out," with the puff direct to then living individuals.

To the present edition have been added several articles contributed by the same writer to the columns of the defunct " Inverness Advertiser." They are interesting to Invernessians as pictures of byegone manners and customs. and as forty years have elapsed since their first appearance in that print, they will be quite new to readers of the present generation.

In 1851 Finlay Maclean proposed publishing, and ad-

Preface to the Second Edition.

vertised, a volume entitled "Memoirs and Incidents of Biography of celebrated Northern Divines of the seventeenth and eighteenth centuries"—these from his father's recollections—but the book was never issued. Two of the articles in the Addenda to the present volume—those on the Rev. Murdo Mackenzie and the Rev. John Porteous—were written for the intended work.

It was the privilege of the editor of this edition to have seen and conversed with the Centenarian. In the autumn of 1851 I was employed as the deputy of a benevolent Inverness lady to convey a sum of money to the old man, who then resided with his daughter as housekeeper in a clay "biggin" in Maclean's Close, Muirtown Street. The old man expressed his thanks for the gift in Gaelic—the language, I think, he best understood—and the rest of the conversation was carried on in the same tongue. At this time, according to Finlay Maclean's statements, his father was in his 1c4th year. His shrivelled-up face, with deep lines, bleared eyes and decrepit form, presented all the appearance of the age claimed for him. He was among the last I saw dressed in a costume that must have been prevalent at one time in Inverness: a blue *cuartear* coat and knee-breeches — both decorated with bright brass buttons— the continuations being deep-ribbed stockings, evidently of home manufacture. On his head he wore one of the long Kilmarnock cowls or nightcaps. A crayon portrait of the Centenarian was taken in this year by a Mr Macarter, drawing master in Dr Bell's Institution. It was a striking likeness of the old man. John Maclean died on the 7th January 1852. The following obituary notice appeared in one our local prints :—

"The oldest inhabitant of Inverness died on Wednesday. He had reached the seldom-equalled age of one hundred and five years. Of the many local changes that have occurred in that time he was a living chronicle. A vigilant observer in his youth, and preserving a retentive memory, which the frailties of old age but slightly impaired, he was able to recount many out-of-the-way anecdotes gathered both from tradition and personal remembrance. He recollected, it is said, the introduction here of most of what are now indispensable requisltes in every town. In his youth there was only a weekly post from the south, by means of foot-runners, over the hills; and when the weather happened to be "coarse" or the runner took "a glass too much," the letters were often several days behind. Afterwards the post was brought thrice a-week by way of Aberdeen. He remembered when the first post-chaise was brought here, which continued for a long time to be the only four-wheeled carriage in the district; and about ten years afterwards (1770) the first cargo of coals was brought to the town, one cargo in the year being sufficient for many years. The people were at first much surprised to find the "black stones" to burn better than the good country peats. At that time there was no bank in the town; the houses were mostly thatched : there was plenty of fish and game, and no lack of smuggled tea and brandy and wine, so that the "merchants and writers" were well off, and their apprentices found them out at night wherever they were, and saw them safe home, though there were no lamps in the streets. The King's Birthday was kept with great splendour; the "town's carpet" was carried out to the Cross, and there the Provost and bailies assembled and drank the claret wine, while the bonfire blazed. He used to speak with great gusto also of the doings when the Judges came round; how a cart-load of peats was burned in the tolbooth to put away the "bad scent," and then after the criminals were tried and condemned—which was nearly synonymous in those days—the Judges, magistrates, and gentry walked up the riverside to the islands in the Ness, crossed in the boat, took salmon out of the cruives, boiled and ate them on the green, with everything else in the style of a grand dinner, and with punch made in a hogshead—nothing less than a hogshead ! The Provost in those days was Mr Hossack. He was called "the kicked Provost," because he was kicked down a stair by General Hawley and his officers, after the battle of Culloden, in consequence of his remonstrating with them on their cruelties to the poor Highlanders. Latterly it afforded him his chief delight to open out on these reminiscences. His declining years were cheered by the charitable assistance of many families in the neighbourhood. His situation and history having been brought under the notice of her Majesty, when a visitor at Ardverikie in 1847, a donation of ten pounds was immediately forwarded to him, enclosed in a letter, which the late Mr Anson, keeper of the Privy Purse, addressed to John Maclean, Esq. It found its appropriate destination, however, and the old man was full proud of the royal courtesy. His remains were interred on Saturday, and a great number of our most influential citizens accompanied them to their last resting-place."

J. N.

Inverness, *Nov.* 1894.

PREFACE TO THE FIRST EDITION.

———o———

"THE Historical and Traditional Sketches" which will be found in the following pages, portions of which had occasionally appeared in the local papers and have been copied into other papers in various parts of Scotland, England, Ireland, India, Australia, and America, are now presented to the public in a more collected and extended form. This is complying with the desires which have been repeatedly expressed by many of the sons of the Gael at home and abroad.

These Sketches have no pretension to literary excellence, nor are they put forward as a full chronological or consecutive history of the families and events to which they refer. Their interest is purely local ; and their merit, if they possess any, is, that they contain historical facts, traits of character, and traditional tales of stirring times and of important personages which have not been presented by any other author.

Of the author, or perhaps I should more properly say, the reciter of these tales, it would not become me, his son, to speak in terms of praise. I may, however, say, without exposing myself to censure, that from his infancy he gave a greedy ear to the recital of old stories ; and when, as at was, and still is, the custom of the country, the fathers, grandfathers, and patriarchs of the town assembled together in the winter evenings and told " the tales of other times," he would sit in the " chimney nook " in wrapt attention listening to their conversation. This predilection of his youth " grew with his growth, and strengthened with his years."

Preface to the First Edition.

An all-merciful and bountiful Creator has been pleased to gift him with good health and a retentive memory. In the course of a life of upwards of a century, he has suffered little bodily illness or mental distress ; and, except so far as his powers are impaired by the natural debility which necessarily attends old age, he still retains the enjoyment of his mental faculties. It may not be out of place to say that one of our Scottish newspapers has lately said of him, " Although the Maitland and Spalding Clubs, and many " antiquarian individuals, have rescued the records of the " country from oblivion, yet John Maclean, the Inverness " historian, by dint of powerful recollection in his own " person, may be said to have eclipsed them." And one of our ablest and most patriotic Chiefs writes—" It is an " unusual blessing conferred on frail and feeble humanity, " that the mind should exercise its unimpaired functions, " and the memory retain its perfect power, when so many " years have worn the fleshly machine in which these work."

In placing these Sketches before the public, I avail myself of the opportunity to express for my father and myself our respectful thanks to the editors of the various newspapers and publications in the old and new worlds who have brought his case before the public, as well as our unfeigned gratitude to the numerous sons of the Gael, "noble, gentle, and simple," at home and abroad, whose benevolence has cast a parting gleam of sunshine on the shortening days of Centenarian.

To his exalted and illustrious Sovereign, who has graciously extended to him her Royal bounty, it would be presumptuous in him to attempt to express his sense of the honour and the benefit she has conferred upon him ; and while his lamp of life shall last, he will offer up his heartfelt supplications for her long, prosperous, and happy reign.

F. M'L.

CONTENTS.

SKETCHES OF
HIGHLAND FAMILIES.

THE MACKINTOSHES OF BORLUM, ETC.

THE Mackintoshes of Borlum were a sept or branch of the Clan Chattan, who had, many centuries ago, as the members of the clan increased, and their power and territory extended, become settled at some distance beyond the immediate neighbourhood of the family possessions of the chief and the country (properly so-called), of the Clan Mackintosh. Like most of the junior branches of the families of Highland chiefs, they had little to depend upon except what might be acquired by craft in council or success in arms; and the Borlum estate became the property of the Mackintoshes without the intervention of a loquacious auctioneer or the officious pedantry of a formal lawyer.* Acting on what was the universal maxim of the age, that "might made right," the Mackintoshes effected the sale by the claymore, took infeftment and sasine of the lands and tenement by the same instrument, without the aid of a notary public, and held possession by wielding, as frequently as occasion required, and with as much power as they could muster, the weapon by the use of which they came into possession.

Situated, as they were, at some distance from the main body of the clan, they formed a sort of picquet or outpost, whose duty it was to watch the movements of the neighbouring clans in the districts of Stratherrick, Urquhart, the Aird, and Ross-shire, and to give intimation to the general body of any intended or attempted encroachment or invasion. It followed from their outward and insulated position, with re-

---

* The statement that being a junior branch of the Clan Mackintosh, they had little to depend upon except what might be acquired by their craft or success in arms is certainly not borne out by the true state of the case. William Mackintosh, *first* of Borlum, was the second son of Lachlan *Mor* Mackintosh, 16th chief; and upon his marriage, 5th July 1595, with Elizabeth Innes of Innermarkie, had the davoch of Clune in Badenoch assigned to him in wadset. When a bachelor Essich was his portion, and prior to his father's death in 1606, he had the davoch of Benchar in Badenoch feued to him by his father, which property remained in the family until 1788. He was thus well provided for.

In addition to Benchar, as above stated, William, in 1610, acquired the estate of Borlum from Campbell of Calder, by purchase, as mentioned in note on page 3.

ference to the main body of the clan, that they had to sustain the first shock of any hostile movement directed against the clan from the west and north, and had to discharge the last or parting blow on the retreat of the enemy; and thus, as with the Borderers in the south, but within a narrower sphere of operation, they were almost unceasingly engaged, either in predatory excursions, or in more regular and formidable attacks. The consequence of occupying so precarious a position, and of the frequent and dangerous conflicts to which it continually exposed them, was, that the Mackintoshes of Borlum became formidable and ferocious, the scourge of the district,—a terror to their foes, and dangerous even to their friends,—a necessary and useful adjunct of the clan, and yet wholly or almost independent of it—certainly beyond the immediate sphere of its control.

The precise period at which the Mackintoshes became possessed of Borlum, is, like most events of the period, involved in considerable uncertainty; but they certainly became proprietors of the estate upwards of four centuries ago, and continued in possession of it beyond the middle of the last century.* From circumstances hereafter detailed, their power,

* Highland tradition is vague and very unsatisfactory to the exact student in history, both as to dates and facts—the latter most frequently exaggerated. In the present case the true date at which the Mackintoshes became possessed of the property of Borlum was 1610, and they disposed of

however, declined, becoming "small by degrees and beautifully less," until at last it altogether ceased, and the estate was transferred to other hands. In 1766 it was purchased by Mr Fraser, a director of the East India Company, a descendant of the ancient family of Foyers,* and father of the present amiable proprietrix, Lady Saltoun.

Throughout the whole of the period during which it was in the possession of the Mackintoshes, it was less or more the resort of the most unprincipled and desperate characters in the country, who found in it a welcome asylum to protect them from consequences of former misdeeds and ready employment for future mischief.† With few exceptions the lairds had acquired a fearful notoriety in the Highlands for the perpetration of every species of crime, in an age and at a time when people were not over-

it in 1760 ; their possession of Borlum thus extended to only 150 years. William Mackintosh, first of Borlum, acquired the property from Campbell of Calder (now the Earl ot Cawdor), the price paid for the same being 3,000 merks. He further acquired Drumboy in Strathnairn and Raitts in Badenoch from the Marquis of Huntly.

* Some years ago this estate was sold, and a portion of it was purchased by the late Mr Fountaine Walker, and is still in possession of the representatives of his family.

† William, first of Borlum, was, during his nephew's minority, acting captain of Clan Chattan, and had the whole clan re-united in one bond of union in 1609. His whole life was spent in the service of three successive chiefs, and no part of his career shows the charge of harbouring worthless characters or broken men to be true.

scrupulous as to the means by which they acquired property, or the manner in which a real or supposed wrong or affront was avenged.

The Mackintoshes of Borlum are now laid in the dust, and the land which once knew them knows them no more; but the remembrance of their iniquities is still associated with the scenes of their former crimes. It is, indeed, difficult to believe, when we look with feelings of pleasure and admiration on the beautiful estate of Lady Saltoun, which is so fertile in cultivation—so tastefully laid out—the home and the hope of so many happy and contented beings, that there, at one time ruled with a rod of iron the Mackintoshes of Borlum, as distinguished for their strength and extent of daring as most of them were for cruelty and crime. Reared up from infancy amidst scenes of blood and danger, they reckoned time by the number and atrocity of their deeds of spoliation and murder, and closed their career in the pursuit of plunder and revenge.

Instead of fruitful fields, yielding laborious but comfortable sustenance to cheerful hundreds, the estate was, when the Mackintoshes possessed it, barren and bare except where it was covered with whins and broom; and where extensive plantations judiciously laid out, intermixed with shrubbery and evergreens, now rise with their variegated foliage enlivening and diversifying the landscape, nothing met the eye but the sterile monotony of heath and stone, with here and there a miserable hut—the temporary residence of daring and restless robbers, the terror of the adjacent country, and the congenial friends and allies of the lairds of Borlum Castle.* " I well remember," adds old John, " the black castle of Borlum, being several times in it on visits to an honest man, whose character was the extreme to that of its occupiers for centuries before." This building was extremely strong—almost impregnable, and was situated on an eminence within a few yards of that on which the present Ness Castle stands.

But what will not time and the industry of man produce? For barren moors and sterile plains, we now see plenty issuing from the pregnant bosom of the earth, and instead of the appalling gloom of Borlum's proud and frowning castle, we behold not a great way off the

---

* The estate was valuable both in respect to fishings and woods. The fir woods were equal to any in the Highlands, and as early as 1631, in an arbitration betwixt Aldourie and Kinchyle of the day, reference is made to " the woods of Borlum." Shaw Mackintosh, sixth of Borlum, sold the estate about 1735 to his relatives Bailies William and Angus Mackintosh of Inverness, but redeemable within a certain number of years. Shaw Mackintosh took steps over twenty years afterwards to redeem, and the bailies complaining, he stated that while Borlum was in their possession and the rents uplifted they had sold as much wood as equalled in value the original price, which still fell to be repaid in full. The name of one of the chief farms--Ballindarroch—shows that oaks abounded. The fishing-pool of Laggan, on the Ness, has been known from the earliest times as affording excellent fishing.

elegant and hospitable mansion of Lady Saltoun—surrounded by its smooth lawn, its serpentine walks and shady bowers. Nor is hers the only mansion, for there are many others besides bearing witness to the progress of civilisation, and the beneficial changes effected generally on the extensive estate of Borlum. But could the castle ruins (traces of which are still visible), the green knolls and running brooks, or the Ness's clear and silvery stream, which winds its way immediately behind, speak the tales of other times, they

> " could a tale unfold whose lightest word
> would harrow up the soul,"

but these witnesses are dumb, and dumb they were doomed to be—yet other witnesses looked on, and thus some account of the foul deeds done have been " handed down from sire to son," for,

> " Murder, tho' it hath no tongue,
> will speak with most miraculous organ."

Of all those who figure in the list of Borlum's lairds, the one who lived about the time of James V. and in the minority of Queen Mary, surpassed them all for fiendish ferocity.*   Like Rob Roy

---

* William, first of Borlum, and his wife, through members of the Athole family, were both of the blood-royal. The charge of cruelty or oppression made here is not borne out on investigation. It is true he got Campbell of Barbeck, who married his brother's widow, kicked out of

(but without any mitigating circumstances to palliate or excuse his conduct), he levied *black mail* on the neighbouring lairds, and unfortunately the favour and protection of the Earl of Huntly, then Governor of the Castle of Inverness (and who invariably lived with Borlum when he came to visit his hunting grounds of Drumashie and other places in the neighbourhood), emboldened him to levy the imposition, and effectually secured him from the consequences. Whoever refused the compulsory payment to Borlum or paid the tribute grudgingly, might look with certainty for a speedy and fearful revenge. Nor was his lady a whit better than her lord. Strong and masculine in person, she was at least as unfortunate as he was in temper, and if possible more savage in revenge.* Never did a greater fiend in female form appear upon the earth, nor was her determination and courage unequal to the execution of her worst purposes ; and of her, in the words of

Dunachton in Badenoch, under aggravating circumstances, but it was the act of the whole family. He also crossed swords with Huntly and Moray in those troublous times, and was engaged in numerous actions offensive and defensive in which the Clan Chattan were concerned.

* It is true that Lady Borlum had been reared in the midst of crime and violence. Her grandfather was murdered in 1584, and her father put to death in Edinburgh for alleged participation in the slaughter of the " bonnie" Earl of Moray, a few days after her marriage in the month of July 1595.

Lady Macbeth it might be truly said—

> "—— I have given to suck ; and know
> How tender 'tis to love the babe that milks me ;
> I would, while it was smiling in my face,
> Have pluck'd my nipple from its boneless gum,
> Aud dash'd the brains out, had I so sworn, as you
> Have done this."

The stories which have been handed down of this fierce couple are numerous as they are frightful. Of these the murder of the venerable Provost Junor of Inverness, was one, and in some degree illustrates their character.* Mrs Mackintosh (or, as the laird's wife is callled in Gaelic, *bean an tighearn,* or the laird's lady), on one occasion went to Inverness, where her visits would be most agreeably dispensed with ; or, in other words, "her absence would be considered good company" by the terrified inhabitants. She was followed by two mischievous imps as train bearers, or lady's henchmen. In the course of her perambulations through the town she was seen by the worthy Provost in a position

> "That mantled to his cheek
> The blush of shame,"

* The author of the "Memorabilia of Inverness" (James Suter) says "that tradition states that about 1618 a Provost of Inverness was murdered by the Mackintoshes of Borlum." Captain Burt, author of "Letters from the North of Scotland," who was in Inverness in 1735, also mentions the tradition as current in his time. To this tradition we can add no information or contradiction. Still powerful though Borlum undoubtedly was, it seems incredible that the town did not resent the murder of their Provost.

and he was so shocked at her rude and indelicate demeanour, that he took courage to reprove her, exclaiming—" O, fie, fie, Lady Borlum." On hearing this, she fixed her kindling eye, glaring with the fiery fierceness of the crouching tiger ere he leaps. More than once she made an effort to speak, but she was choked with passion—her heart was too full " of pride, of rage and malice "—all her faculties were wound up, and her tongue refused its office— she stood immoveable as a marble. At length, making a desperate effort, and raising herself to her full height, she said, as she slowly turned away her flaming eye, " You shall dearly pay for this," and passed on. Her determined but subdued tone, her flashing eye, that plainly indicated

> " ——— The coming events
> That cast their shadows before,"

impressed the decent, sober, but in this case indiscreet magistrate, with a presentiment of future revenge.

Lady Borlum having inwardly sworn (and she seldom swore an oath that it might be broken), that the Provost's death alone should satisfy her revenge, proceeded homewards, ruminating over her wrong, and concocting schemes for the execution of her diabolical purpose. Borlum was not at home on her return, and did not return for sometime thereafter ; but in the interval the violence of her fury had rather increased than diminished, and she hailed her lord's return as the speedy harbinger of death; and when she beheld, as she did at the first glance by his dark and stern look lowering brow, and compressed lips, that he too was in no very amiable humour, she welcomed him with more than ordinary joy, and he was scarcely seated, when she poured her tale, with such exaggerations as her malice suggested, into an ear as greedy to hear as she to tell; and when she had finished, she said that nothing could or would satisfy her but the old man's death. To this Borlum, without reflecting on the matter—for in his estimation it would have been beneath him to trouble himself a moment in reflecting on such a trifling affair as the death of a burgher—at once assented. The Provost's death being thus agreed upon, the how, by whom, and where, were the next questions to be settled.

Having obtained, rather than won the laird's assent, which she had asked more as a matter of course than as a thing essential, the gloomy pair sat down to supper. Both intent on separate purposes, they partook of the evening meal in silence. The moor, the valley, and the stream supplied the supper. The moors of Stratherrick furnished the game, the rich flavoured and sweet tasted mutton was taken in foray from some of the estates in the neighbourhood, and the prolific Ness yielded the salmon. The strong pot-ale that overtopped the rich gilt flaggons that lined the board was home brewed; the genuine mountain-dew that filled the capacious vessel that occupied the centre of the table was distilled in Abriachan's most secret shade; and the generous and exhilarating products of the vine, which, in long-necked bottles adorned with silver tops, graced the table, were a present from an offshoot of the family, who had been forced to fly to foreign climes, but, who, amidst the excitement of foreign wars, the charms of France and Italy, and the fascinating influence of more civilised and more enchanting manners, never forgot the land of his birth,

> "The birthplace of valour,
> The country of worth."

The silent gloomy supper over, and the dishes removed, the congenial pair moved towards the fire. Long and silently they sat. Both were wrapt up in alternate musings of past mischief and future revenge. In the bosoms of both, the compunctions of conscience for a moment pricked the soul, and in the next, from an innate love of fiendish self-condemnation for having even for a moment listened to the still small voice of reason, their hearts were kindled into revenge— their souls were dark—their purposes Satanic; and these two, whom no magic cord of love did bind, who felt not the uniting bond of man and wife, nor the indescribable co-union and co-existence which parents feel when children bless the marriage-knot—these two, who had never known the secret mystery by which in friendship, love, and affection soul communicates with soul, were linked and bound in inseparable and constant union in the dark impulses of mischief, and the self-consuming gratification of revenge.

For hours they sat, wrapt in black thought and desperate purpose, until the flickering light of the dying fire, shedding an uncertain and party coloured glare on their recumbent forms, and unmoved but fearful countenances, aroused them from contemplation to talk as well as think of bloody purposes. Lady Borlum retold her story and urged her lord to revenge the insult which had been offered to her. The laird listened with attention, and signified his wish to hear how she proposed to gratify her desire. Various were the schemes proposed, and long the consultation continued. At length it was determined—for nothing else would satisfy the lady—that as the Provost would be taking his customary walk the following evening, he should be despatched by their two sons Unless his life was taken away by the hand of one of her own flesh and blood, her vengeance, she said, would not be half satisfied; and her husband, although he had urged a bolder course, at last consented, and they retired to bed—to bed, but not to sleep, for what sleep can ever reach the tortuous restlessness of a foul mind, or silence the damning testimony of a guilty conscience?

On the following morning, Provost Junor

rose as hearty and unconcerned as if the incident of the previous day had not occurred,—his
heart was at ease, no tremulous yearnings of
conscience obtruded themselves to disturb his
mind ; nor did one passing thought of the previous day's encounter with Lady Borlum arise
to disturb his serenity and self-complacency.
That encounter, terrible certainly at the time,
(and especially so to a man of his quiet habits
and peaceable disposition,) had ruffled his
temper and very much frightened him, but it
soon passed away, and in an hour afterwards, the
happy, good-natured official might be seen receiving and retailing the gossip of the town with
his usual cheerfulness and good humour—his
fright had entirely melted away, and like last
year's snow, left no trace of its temporary existence behind. On the succeeding day he got up
at his usual hour, and paid his accustomed formal
attention to the cleanliness and neatness of his
magisterial person ; his square hat was carefully
brushed, his wig was made trim and neat, his
broad flapped coat was well dusted, his knee-
breeches—with fringes above the knee, as was
he fashion of the time—were stainless ; nor were
his "*brocan dhu*" forgotten, although Day and
Martin were yet unborn. Thus attired, and
ample justice done to a good breakfast, he took
his gold-mounted official staff and went forth to
attend to his private business (that of a skin
merchant), and his magisterial functions. Having paid the requisite attention to his "ain"

private affairs, which, as a prudent and well-
doing citizen it behoved him to do, as he was
wont to say, he applied himself to the discharge
of his public duties with well-meaning zeal, and
with a pomposity which was somewhat foreign
to his nature, and which therefore became with
him at least questionable grace, but which he
thought the dignity of the office made it necessary for him to assume. His business being
over, he returne to his house about mid-day—
partook of the plain and substantial dinner
which was placed before him with a hearty appe-
tite and a contented mind. After dinner he
enjoyed his nap, and relished his chat as usual—
no cloud crossed his brow, no apprehensions of
coming evil agitated his mind, nor was his heart
touched by any unpleasant forebodings. Time
passed on ; morning, noon, and evening came
and went, and the shades of night began to fall
gradually around, nature seemed as if drawing
together the curtains of repose,—the world
was calm and still, not the profound stillness
of the midnight hour, but that soothing quietness which imparts a tender melancholy to
the mind, making it serious without austerity,
and contemplative without effort, and which
touches and expands the better promptings of
the heart. It was somewhat later than eight
o'clock, as the guileless Provost left the town
and directed his steps towards the Gaic or
Drumden, now called, from the circumstance of
the Black Watch having been embodied and en-

camped there, Campfield.   At this period there was no regular road between Inverness and Campfield, nor did the face of the hill westward of the town bear any traces of cultivation. It was then bare and sterile, although it is now adorned with elegant patches of garden, shrubbery, and plantation, and beautified by handsome villas.   The irregular broken footway wound its course along the margin of the river, until near the present water-house, when it diverged a little towards the base of the hill, and proceeded up the hollow between Drummond and Campfield. Along this path the Provost was in the habit of taking his walk in the summer and autumn evenings, and being a regular and exact man, he almost invariably went and returned at the same hour.   On the particular evening to which allusion has been made, he proceeded on his walk with slow and steady pace, enjoying the solemn but not oppressive stillness which reigned around, now gazing in devout contemplation of the moveless sky, anon following with his eye the homeward flight of some wearied traveller of the feathered tribe; and when the eye could no longer trace his form on the darkening horizon, and attracted by the rippling of the stream as it broke over the stones and pebbles which obstructed its progress, he looked in silent admiration on the ceaseless flow of the waters of his own bright river, now tinged with the darkening hues of the clouds above, as it swept on in its course to join the ocean,

But to return to Borlum Castle. As the soft golden light of the setting sun was taking a last parting kiss of the western mountain tops, and the black clouds, which began gradually descending, as if to relieve the rays of the setting sun announced the approach of the crime-begetting night, the sons of Borlum were called to their mother's presence. Though bred in a school where scruples formed no part of the discipline, yet the young men were somewhat staggered when informed by their *loving* mother of the business they were to perform. Although sufficiently inured to crime, to blunt, if not entirely to eradicate any compunctious yearnings of humanity, they still retained something of the buoyancy and chivalry of youth not to feel some repugnance to commit a deed so foul and so unmanly ; and, accordingly, took the liberty of telling her that they felt great reluctance to obey her commands, and that it would oblige them if she appointed some other instruments of vengeance. Curbing her wrath against such disobedience, and the better to accomplish her purpose, she disclosed to them the provocation she had received. But instead of the recital producing the anticipated effect, the sons could scarce refrain from indulging in open laughter.

The mother's quick and eager eyes saw this irreverence, and her wrath was rising into fury— a fury which the sons, bold and desperate as they were, could not face without fear, and which they no sooner perceived than they yielded an ungracious acquiescence, and with little loss of time departed on their mission. As they reached the verge of the eminence which overlooks the pathway, they beheld the Provost at some distance advancing with easy step towards them. They remained concealed until he had gained the summit of the hill, and when but a few yards from them, he paused to take breath after the ascent, and survey the familiar scene before him. The assassins sprung from their lurking-place with the agility and ferocity of their race, and ere the worthy magistrate could recognise his murderers, he breathed his last, pierced in several places by their daggers.

Thus foully fell, by the hand of Borlum's ruthless sons, and at the instigation of their more bloody mother, between his sixtieth and seventieth year, Provost Junor of Inverness—a skin merchant by trade—a wealthy and respectable citizen—an able magistrate, and a kind, inoffensive man. After the accomplishment of this horrid and unprovoked tragedy, the brothers removed the body further down the hill, and hid it in whin bushes. Having thus performed their mother's stern command, they returned with all possible haste to tell the pleasing tale. During their absence, Lady Borlum was unusually restless and uneasy—they had now been absent two hours, which seemed to her as so many days—she looked out with eager and watchful eyes, until the thickening darkness made further watching unavailing, and, at length, her patience was exhausted, and misgivings thick and strong came crowding upon her mind, that the resolutions of her sons had failed, or that some unlucky accident had interposed between her purpose and its accomplishment— that the attempt had been made and the deed not done, or that unlooked-for aid came to the old man's rescue, and murdered those who were to be his murderers. These, and a thousand other conjectures, came rushing upon her with the rapidity of thought, and made her almost mad. At length, however, she heard a knocking at the outer iron gate of the Castle, when her heart beat with increased velocity and violence ; her breathing became quick and difficult, her eyes burned and her head swam—bound up in the feverishness of anxiety and the intensity of suspense, she stood motionless, and when her two sons entered the room, and pointed to their unsheathed daggers covered with blood as the most eloquent and impressive description of the work they had done—she turned her fiendish and glazing eyes upon the daggers, and giving a scream of fiendish joy, fell upon the floor.

Here, for the present, we must leave this crime-begetting haunt and return to the house of mourning and of woe. The Lady of Borlum was not the only one who on this fatal night felt anxiety and alarm. Ten o'clock came, a

more than usually late hour for the Provost to
be out, and yet he returned not, but his wife,
though somewhat alarmed at his absence, was
still confident he might have met some neighbour, and gone home with him to crack over a
" *cogie* " or two of ale ; or he might be engaged
on some council business ; but when eleven
o'clock came and the Provost not returning,
she became restless, and some shadows of
alarm began to cross her mind ; still she sat
without communicating her uneasiness to any
one. Midnight brought not back Provost
Junor, and the dark forebodings which the
hushed silence of the midnight hour is apt to
bring to more easy minds than Mrs Provost
Junor's, then began to settle into alarm and
terror. Morning arrived and yet no traces of
her loving and affectionate husband. The tidings of the sudden disappearance of the worthy
Provost excited the greatest sensation and
alarm for his safety, and numerous were the
conjectures whispered about him in the town
and neighbourhood, but none which could afford
any consolation to his anxious wife. The
Council now assembled, and dark hints were
freely exchanged as to his mysterious fate.
After many fruitless inquiries, it was at length
resolved to search along the line of his usual
evening walk—as more than one had seen him
going in that direction, but none saw him
return. This search was prosecuted with great
diligence and minuteness, and at length the

mutilated body of the chief magistrate was found huddled together under a whin bush—his hat and stick at some distance off. The townspeople crowded around the body, and there was not a dry eye present nor a silent tongue. Every one remembered something to his credit, and as the body was carefully and solemnly carried to the town, the praises of the departed magistrate were feelingly sung amidst tears and lamentations by his sorrowing fellow-citizens. *

An investigation was immediately entered into for the purpose of discovering and punishing the perpetrators of this foul deed. Various circumstances were discovered calculated to bring strong suspicions on the Borlum family, and in a day or two after the murder there remained no room to doubt, what all from the very first suspected, that the assassins were the sons of Borlum. Meetings after meetings were held to bring them to punishment, but the Town Council, although eager enough to avenge the death of their chief magistrate, dreaded the ferocity and power of Borlum (who was himself a member of Council), the more particularly

---

* The story of Provost Junor's murder is related with all the minutiæ of the modern journalist—the feelings of all concerned in the foul deed, and their conversations, and even their thoughts so detailed, is wonderful! But we doubt not that Mr Finlay Maclean (the son of the Inverness Centenarian), who wrote this narrative, drew largely on his own imagination for the particulars set forth in his pages.

as he was backed by the friendship and power of the Earl of Huntly, at the time exercising almost regal authority in the north, and by whom, as has been already noticed, black Mackintosh of Borlum had been protected from the consequences of his evil deeds. The Council, therefore, however reluctantly, were obliged to abandon the idea of punishing the assassins, and all they could do to show their respect for the deceased Provost and their detestation and horror of his murderers, was to pass a resolution that no member of the Borlum family should ever be eligible to a seat in the Town Council of Inverness—a resolution which was ever after during their occupancy of Borlum and Raitts most strictly adhered to.*

Not long after the tragedy of Provost Junor's death, another victim fell a sacrifice to the bloodthirsty vengeance of the Lady of Borlum. As was usual in every laird's family at this time, there lived in that of Borlum a female servant, whose principal business was to bake the family

---

* Subsequently to that period, however, more than one descendant of this ill-fated family sat in the Council. and also filled the office of Provost with credit and honour —gentlemen who excelled in humanity, and who delighted in doing good to their poor fellow-creatures ; but this was after Borlum and Raitts had passed into more honest hands and after the last laird of Borlum had fled the country.

[The preceding note is by Mr Maclean, the author of the work, but it is not correct. The story that no Borlum or any of his descendants should thereafter be eligible to hold a seat in the Town Council, modified, as alleged, after the

bread, and who from this circumstance, and her shortness of stature, obtained the *soubriquet* of " *Ipac Bheag na Brecaig,*" or Little Isabel of the bannocks. On the evening on which Provost Junor was murdered, Ipac Bheag had been sent on some errand to Inverness, and as she was returning, became an unwilling and accidental witness of the murderous deed done by her master's sons, and partaking of the weakness which has at all times characterised her sex, she could neither get rest, or peace of mind, until she found some one in whom she could confide, and unburthen her mind of the dangerous and fearful load with which it was charged. Relying on the fidelity and integrity of a fellow-servant, Ipac, still with great reluctance, unbosomed herself to this person, and revealed to her all she had seen—the revelation at the same time lightening herself of the burden which agonised her whole frame. In a few days thereafter this *confidante* made it no point of conscience to betray poor Ipac to her master and mistress. From that moment her fate was sealed. Neither the laird, his lady, or their sons, cared much about the fact of a witness having been present to bear testimony to their villany. The Provost's murder had been

estate of Borlum was sold, is inaccurate, for no such resolution can be found on the record ; and William and Angus Mackintosh, grandsons of the second Borlum by a younger son sat in the Council, and also as magistrates, long before Borlum was sold. —ED.]

clearly traced to them, and could not be denied. It was, therefore, a matter of perfect indifference to them, whether or not there were any witnesses who could give direct and positive evidence as to their guilt. They depended not on their power to hide the truth, but on their power to shield themselves from its consequences. But indifferent, as they consequently were, as to who saw or did not see the act committed, it was another, and a very different affair, that one of their servants, eating their own bread, having many opportunities of observing their every act, should publish so important a secret and blab their guilt to the world. For this imprudence, in the estimation of the Borlum family, one of the most heinous of crimes, Ipac's death was resolved on. On the day after it came to the knowledge of the family that she had acted an unguarded part she was sent on a pretended message to Bona Ferry, a distance of about two miles westward from the castle, and when returning late in the evening she was waylaid, and most barbarously murdered. To conceal murder, fresh murder must be committed ; thus it ever is. The mind once habituated to crime, all the restraints of morality, religion, and of conscience are overthrown—guilt becomes familiar, and conscience callous

"I am so steeped in guilt, that
I may as well go through as turn back."

For many, many years afterwards, Ipac's

ghost was seen to " haunt the lone vale," wandering up and down the banks of the river, and its doleful lamentations were heard within the walls of Borlum Castle. The very herds who were wont to tend their sheep and cattle along the banks of the Ness, were so familiar with Ipac Bheag's wraith, that its mournful cries latterly became a signal to them to return home with their charge.

We have already mentioned that the Borlum family were the terror and scourge of the neighbouring lairds. However, Maclean of Dochgarroch, who had experienced much annoyance and oppression, made a bold attempt to resist Borlum's overbearing power, and set his threats at defiance, which so maddened him, that to be revenged he directed his son, and about thirty of his vassals and dependents, to proceed to Dochgarroch House, raze it to the ground, and destroy everything belonging to his mortal enemy. The good and worthy proprietor of Dochgarroch, being apprised of this force having marched, and the object in view, but ignorant of their number, sent twelve brave and faithful clansmen to watch young Borlum and his desperate companions in arms. On the north bank of the river, a little to the west of the ancient Castle of Spiritual, the little band of the Macleans met the more numerous one of Borlum advancing at a rapid pace ; no words were exchanged, no explanation demanded ; both parties knew each other too well to require information as to each other's mission. Undismayed by the disparity in numbers, the Macleans with their claymores and Lochaber axes, rushed upon their opponents. The Macleans maintained their ground most gallantly, diminishing their foes at every blow, and ultimately forced them into the river, where, up to their middle in the water, the battle was fought with unabated fury and deadly animosity for a considerable time. The clear stream was reddened with the blood of the slain and wounded for some distance from the spot of combat. So brave and determined were the Macleans, with the recollections of the wrongs and oppressions of their foes fresh in their memory, and the desperate enterprise upon which they were, that every blow inflicted added fresh vigour to the resolute arm dealing it, and they firmly resolved, that before yielding to the laird of Borlum's son, every one should be " with his back to the field, and his face to the foe." Such was the undaunted courage and deadly determination evinced by both parties, that the combatants did not separate until almost annihilated. Of the gallant little handful of the Macleans, three only survived to tell the result of this bloody fray ; and among the eight of the Mackintoshes who escaped was Borlum's wounded son.*

* The story of the fight between the Mackintoshes of Borlum and the Macleans of Dochgarroch is apocryphal, as no such tradition exists amongst the representatives of

Tidings of this affair spread like wildfire through the country, and the neighbouring lairds were secretly rejoiced at the repulse the Mackintoshes thus received, and the undaunted bravery displayed by the few sons of Clan Gillean was the theme of their praise. This battle brought some discredit on the Mackintoshes. Nevertheless for a time they continued to advance in importance, not only from the number of their vassals, and the daring and desperate character of the laird and his followers, but also from the favour and countenance extended to the laird of that day by the Earl of Huntly, whose power and authority in the north, as already stated, was of itself a sufficient shield. But soon afterwards they gradually declined ; their followers became few—they were less fortunate in their adventures—and their power and importance became more limited ; it was getting "short by degrees, and beautifully less."

It was supposed that the laird of Borlum, in

these families. It seems to be confounded with an undoubted fight at Castle Spiritual which took place at a much earlier date (15th century) than that mentioned in the above text, when the Macleans were in possession of Urquhart, and before they were settled in Dochgarroch. The fight was beween the Camerons of Lochiel and the Macleans. The atrocities committed by the Camerons on this occasion led to a belief that the old castle of Bona was haunted, hence it became known as " Castle Spiritual." (See *Mackay's " Urquhart and Glenmoriston,"* 1894, page 94, etc.)

return for the favour and protection which he had uniformly received from the Earl of Huntly, was indirectly implicated in the betrayal of the Chief of Clan Chattan to the Earl, who had him executed, and that in revenge for this real, or supposed betrayal, the estate of Borlum suffered some part of the punishment which the clan inflicted on those who were implicated in the affair.*   Be this as it may, it is nevertheless certain that from this time the family power began to decline ; but although decreasing in power, the successive lairds lost little of that ferocity which had obtained for them so bad a notoriety, nor did they degenerate from their forefathers in their deportment in battle, or their avidity for crime.†   It is, however, but right to

---

* William, the fifteenth chief of Clan Chattan, was executed in August 1550, and as the *first* Borlum was his grandson — born long after this date — the folly of this accusation is evident.

† The history of the various successive lairds of Borlum does not bear out the charges of ferocity and criminality here made, as already shown in the case of the first Borlum.

Lachlan, the *second* Borlum, who first married the widow of Sir Lachlan Mackintosh, thereby incurred the deep resentment of her sons William Mackintosh of Mackintosh and Lachlan Mackintosh of Kinrara to such a degree that all his life he struggled with poverty, living chiefly in Badenoch, without power to hurt or oppress any one.

William, the *third* of Borlum, married Mary Baillie of Dunean.   He held a prominent position from 1652 to 1717.   He lived chiefly at Borlum, where he died.   No charge of cruelty or oppression has been ever stated against him.   The character given of him by certain Macphersons in Badenoch shows how well he discharged his duties to his employer the Duke of Gordon (see *Spalding Club Miscel-*

except from this sweeping condemnation, the most celebrated member of the family, Brigadier General Mackintosh, or, as he was more familiarly called, " Old Borlum," who, though possessing much of the sterness, had very little of the cruelty of his forefathers. His indomitable courage, enterprising character, and unshaken constancy were conspicuously displayed in his daring expedition across the Forth—his skilful and masterly retreat to Kelso—his bravery at Preston—his escape from Newgate, and his subsequent flight to France, which have left for him a proud name in the annals of his country that in some measure redeems the character of his family from that infamy which their cruelty deservedly obtained for them.*

From various causes, some of them, no doubt, arising from the civil wars in which the Borlum family took an active part, in favour of the unfortunate Stuarts, the family was, in

---

lany, vol. iv. page 165), as illustrated by the attempted murder of his successor Glenbucket by the Macphersons, as noted by Burt and others.

* Brigadier Mackintosh, the *fourth* of Borlum, has been excepted by Maclean from the general condemnation brought against his family. To readers of the history of the rising of the " 1715 " it is unnecessary to detail the career of the Brigadier—the only chief in the Jacobite army who displayed generalship. The very street ballads of the time were partial to this gallant soldier—

> " Mackintosh was a soldier brave,
> And of his friends he took his leave ;
> Toward Northumberland he boldly came,
> Marching with gallant men of his name," etc.

the time of Edward, the last laird, very greatly
diminished, and somewhere about the year
1760, the extensive estate of Borlum was sold.
It had been in possession of the Mackintoshes
for upwards of three hundred years, never likely
to be again the property of any of that ilk.
The estate of Raitts or Raitles, in Badenoch,
was still held by them, where Edward, the last
laird, resided, whose character in a great measure corresponded with that of too many of his
ancestors.

From the period at which Provost Junor was
assassinated by the Mackintoshes of Borlum,
the power of that family gradually declined.
The Clan Mackintosh, whose interest it was to
keep up a good understanding with the burgh of
Inverness ; and who, besides, felt the natural
repugnance which was entertained, even in those
unscrupulous days, to the perpetration of murder, under circumstances not connected with the
interest or credit of the clan, and which could
not be justified by any of the (so-called) "laws
of honour and clanship" which prevailed in the
Highlands at the time, were not slow in expressing their disapprobation of the heartless and
cowardly act. The apparent independence of
the rest of the clan, which the lairds of Borlum
had, for a long period, arrogated to themselves,
arising from their isolated position, their previous services to the clan, their direct family
power and influence ; and above all, the countenance which they received from, and the

services which they rendered to the all-powerful family of Huntly, at length subjected them, not only to the suspicion of the clan but exposed them to the secret hatred and open hostility of the chiefs of Clan Chattan. The consequence of such a combination of adverse circumstances was then, as it would be now, that those who would be the followers of the lairds of Borlum, through fear, gradually became emboldened, as the power of the latter declined, to throw off their yoke ; and that those who followed them from interested and merely mercenary motives, diminished in number as the influence of the clan perceptibly lessened, and the prospects of reward became more uncertain.

But these causes, powerful and sufficient as they appear, were not the only ones to which we are to attribute the fall of this family. There were higher, more potent and less fallible causes at work, the existence of which, in the decline and fall of the family, it would be as impious to deny as the attempt to describe the mode in which they operated would be rash and presumptuous. *The Christian believes, and the infidel feels and fears, the certainty of retributive justice.* Its progress may be accelerated or protracted, but nothing is so certain in physical science, in the investigations of the astrologer or the chemist, nor even in the certainty of the connection which must exist between cause and effect, as that justice will be done even upon earth ; and that He who gives the assurance that the bread which is thrown upon the waters, shall, after many days, return with increase, will as certainly punish " the iniquities of the fathers upon the children, even to the third and fourth generation."

Exposed to the operation of these agencies, and writhing under the withering influences of the unconcealed dislike of the clan, the openly expressed disgust of their neighbours, and what was still more galling to their feelings and pride, being openly bearded and defied by the worthless wretches who had been called into importance by their power and patronage, the lairds of Borlum, as they declined in power, became more remorseless. As the means of committing injustice became more limited, their passions became more fiendish and debased ; their infamy increased as their degradation was made more manifest; their moral turpitude became impervious as loss succeeded loss, and degradation followed degradation, until at last, like the ruined gambler of modern times, who had become involved in the vortex of play, and who resorts to one unfair trick after another, as his means melt away, despised and scouted by his former associates, he is forced to seek other company, among whom he may play a still more disreputable part,—the Mackintoshes gradually fell from their feudal power and lordly splendour, and were forced to leave

" the land o'er which they ruled supreme,"

and take up their residence on the estate of Raitts, in Badenoch, and sink from the dignified position of lairds levying black mail, to the less honourable profession of " taking purses, and going by the moon and seven stars." *

At Raitts, or, as it is now called, Belleville, the last laird of Borlum, Edward Mackintosh, resided. In many respects he excelled most of his forefathers in ferocity, and was one of the most daring robbers that ever lived in the Highlands of Scotland. Within a mile and a half of the mansion-house there is an artificial cave in which he and his band found a convenient and secure lurking place from which to sally forth to rob travellers of their purses, and sometimes of their lives. In a recently published statistical account of Inverness-shire, will be found mention made of this cave. It states that " the excavation, when entire, amounted to 145 yards—was artificially built round with dry stones, and covered with large gray flags, by a desperate band of depredators, commonly

---

* Following the notes on page 29, it may be stated. in reply to the assertion here made, that Lachlan, *fifth* of Borlum, eldest son of Brigadier Mackintosh, had to seek his fortune in early youth in New England, and perished at sea. In 1720 he was admitted a free burgess of Inverness.

Shaw, *sixth* of Borlum, brother of Lachlan, parted with Borlum, on a redeemable right, in 1734 and the family never returned to Borlum. Shaw retired to Raitts, and married Jean Menzies of Woodhill, county of Perth, and after her death lived a retired life.

called *Clannmagilleanoidh.** " Over the cave
was erected a turf cottage, or dwelling-house,
such as the people of the country inhabited at
the time, the inmates of which enjoyed the confidence of the occupiers of the cave ; were the
depositaries of their secrets, and participated
along with them in the spoil of the Macphersons.

* We give the full particulars from the account of the
parish of Alvie in the *Statistical Account of* 1842 :—" It
is not certain to what particular clan these depredators be-
longed.   Instigated by implacable hatred against the Macphersons, on account of some deadly feud, they secretly
dug the cave, which is called, after their name, *Uaigh
Clannmhicgillenaoidh*, as a place of concealment, from
which they occasionally sallied forth in the night time
to steal and to slaughter the cattle of the Macphersons,
wherever they could be found. . . . The Macphersons finding the number of their cattle daily diminishing, made a
strict search after them, but for a long time without effect.
At length appearances were noticed about the hut erected
over the cave, which excited a strong suspicion that the
lurking place of these depredators could not be very distant
from that hut.   This suspicion was increased by the inhos-
pitable churlishness of the landlord, who contrary to the
custom of the times, would permit no stranger to lodge for
a single night in his house.   Accordingly the Macphersons
sent one of their number as a spy in the garb of a beggar
to solicit a night's lodging in the suspected hut : and feign-
ing illness from a fit of the gravel, the beggar was allowed
to remain in a barn or outhouse for the night.   The beggar
being thus disposed of, the most active preparations commenced within the house for a sumptuous entertainment ;
and the feast being prepared, a large flag was raised in the
centre of the house, on which *Clannmhicgillenaoidh* came
out, feasted on the Macphersons' choicest beef, along with
the inmates of the house, and then spent the remainder of

In the now thriving village of Kingussie, in the immediate vicinity of the haunt of the Mackintoshes and their associates, there were at the time of which we write, but a few miserable, straggling huts, whose proximity to the cave imposed no check upon Borlum's movements, but rather aided, than obstructed him in his bad and bold career ; for it not unfrequently happened that travellers, whilst refreshing themselves at the little public-house in the village, were joined by some of Edward's associates, who on such occasions kept the mountain dew in circulation, so as to make easier victims ; and when the unfortunate traveller sallied forth to renew his journey, under disadvantage of a glass too much, some of the gang were sure to waylay him and ease him of his cash.　For a long time, Edward and his lawless crew conducted their depredations with caution and

the night in search of a fresh supply.　The beggar observed all that passed through an aperture on the side of the hut, and returned to report what he had seen.　In consequence of the discovery thus made, the Macphersons collected a strong party on the following night, seized and massacred the whole band of *Clannmhicgillenaoidh*, in the cave, demolished the hut erected over it, and thus put an end to those freebooters, and to all their depredations.　The pretended beggar by whom *Clannmhicgillenaoidh* were betrayed was called Ian Mac Eoghaiwn, or John Macewan, and the tribe of the Macphersons descended from him are distinguished by the appellation of *Sliochd Ian Mhiceoghainn*, that is, John Macewan's descendants.　It is said that all this tribe have ever since been peculiarly liable, at some period of life, to be more or less afflicted with gravel."

secresy * ; but, emboldened by impunity and success, they at length became recklessly daring, put the law at defiance, and committed crimes of the greatest enormity in open day, insomuch that that the whole district was alarmed, and accounts of their crimes spread over the kingdom, and prevented travellers from going by that road. Nevertheless, there were no means taken to suppress the daring outrages daily committed by this band of highwaymen. On one occasion, Edward being informed by some of his satellites that Mr Macgregor, factor or chamberlain for the laird of Grant, was collecting the rents from the tenants in Glen-Urquhart, thought it no bad concern to lay in wait for his return in the lonely, wild, and craggy rocks of Slochmuicht. Accordingly, he set out alone, thinking, being well armed, that he himself would easily overcome the worthy factor, and accomplish the object sought, viz., to rob him of all his money. In that obscure and wild retreat, he remained two days in the utmost anxiety. Mr Macgregor at last made his appearance mounted on a Highland pony, accompanied by a trusty gillie. Edward Mackintosh immediately sprung from his hiding-place, levelled and fired his piece, but as the factor anticipated that Ned Mackintosh or some of his party would be on the look out for securing a rich booty, he took the precaution of having himself

---

* The period was less than a year.

and his servant well armed ; consequently, when the shot was fired, fortunately with no effect, the factor, in the true spirit of his namesake Rob Roy, returned the fire, and then challenged Ned to a fight with claymore or pistol. Edward finding he was thus discovered, precipitately fled to his place of concealment, like a tiger disappointed of his prey, and Mr Macgregor was allowed to proceed in safety with his wallet well filled with bank notes, gold and silver to Castle Grant. All were not so fortunate as Mr Macgregor, for some time thereafter, a poor wandering and aged pedlar, who, besides supplying the surrounding country with his wares, was also the newsvendor and chronicler of the events, and who, from his honest principles and inoffensive humour, had become a favourite for many years with high and low, and familiar with all, had been waylaid, robbed, and murdered, as it was conjectured, by Ned Mackintosh or some of his companions, and his body afterwards buried in the sands of Speyside. Justice, though it may for a time be eluded, and sometimes frustrated, will eventually prevail, for

" —— many a crime, deem'd innocent on earth,
Is registered in heaven ; and there no doubt
Have each a record with a curse annexed."

A drover of the name of John M'Rory, *alias* M'Farquhar, from the neighbourhood of Redcastle, Ross-shire, who had been for many years in the habit of driving cattle south by the Perth

road, and was reputed wealthy, was one time
returning home from the southern markets,
where he had been disposing of his cattle, and
when two or three miles north of the now
flourishing, clean, and populous village of Kingussie, was waylaid by Edward and (as he
said) his illegitimate brother Alexander. Mac-
farquhar, or as he was more commonly called,
M'Rory (by which last name we will abide),
was rather an ugly customer to have to do with,
and in a fair stand up fight, would have paid
any man in as fair a manner as he had got.

Edward, who was some distance in advance
of his brother, commanded M'Rory to deliver
up his purse, otherwise his life must pay the
forfeit. M'Rory did not much relish either the
proposition or the alternative ; but ere he had
time to speak, Edward's hand had grasped his
throat, and with the other seized the bridle of
drover's horse. M'Rory was fully sensible of
his perilous situation. Alexander was hasten-
ing to his brother's assistance, and was not
many yards off, when, to increase his fear and
anxiety, the drover heard the tread of approaching footsteps caused no doubt by the advance
of some more of the same gang. There was no
time to lose—everything depended upon expedition and self-command. The drover raised
his hand to his throat, as if to grasp the oppressive hand of his antagonist, but in reality to
cut his handkerchief with his knife. This done
he passed his hand to the reins, and cut them ;

then clutching Ned by the throat, hurled him to a distance of some yards, and at the same moment applying the whip to his garron, made " twa pair of legs " worth one pair of hands. Bending his body down as far as possible on the neck of his nag, off he went at full speed. He did not, however, altogether escape scaithless, for ere he could get beyond the range of their fire the bullets whistled, as he afterwards declared, " like hailstones aboot his lugs," some of which even penetrated his clothes, particularly his greatcoat, but fortunately no further. But for the thick quality and superabundant quantity of his apparel, Jock M'Rory might bid adieu to all terrestrial affairs. Upon his arrival in Inverness, he called upon the Sheriff, Mr Campbell of Delnies (a gentleman to whom access at all times was easily obtained), to whom he communicated the particulars of his unpleasant encounter.

A warrant was immediately issued and placed in the hands of an officer, for the apprehension of Edward Mackintosh and his brother Alexander, they being the only persons M'Rory had ever seen and could identify. Although the officer received injunctions to apprehend the Mackintoshes with the utmost secrecy and despatch, yet Edward contrived to get information of the warrant for his apprehension having been issued, and the directions for executing it given to the officer to whom it was entrusted, when he summoned a full attendance of his companions in crime to the house of Raitts, where he entertained them to a sumptuous supper and a splendid ball, and early next morning took his departure for the south, escorted a number of miles by his comrades.

He remained in private for some weeks in the house of a friend in Edinburgh, and afterwards made good his escape to France, where, previous to the Revolution, he attained to some eminence in the army of that country, but his ultimate fate is unknown.* Whether he took part in the tragedy which Europe beheld with horror and amazement enacted in a country holding the first place in the march of civilisation, and in the bloody actions of which he was, by his recklessness and ferocity, so well calculated to take a prominent part, is also unknown. The star of his house arose amidst the darkness and the barbarity of the feudal times, and attained, with surprising velocity, a high altitude in power and crime. In its progress it produced terror and destruction. The increasing light of advancing civilisation gradually diminished its power, until, after more than three

* Edward, the *seventh* and last Borlum, succeeded about 1770. His conduct cannot be justified, nor even explained, except on the ground of criminal mental aberration. Indeed an examination of the evidence produced on the trial in 1773 exhibits such utter folly, such a want of ordinary precaution, considering the dangerous mode of life practised, as to be simply incredible. The estates of Raitts and Benchar were judicially sold in 1788, many years after Edward Mackintosh's flight, his creditors being paid in full.

hundred years, it sank for ever, and their name,

" Doubly dying shall go down
To the vile dust from whence it sprung,
Unwept, unhonoured, and unsung."

Although Edward Mackintosh, laird of Borlum, as already mentioned, succeeded in effect-
ing his escape, yet his illegitimate brother,
Alexander, was apprehended and conveyed to
Inverness, and, in due time,* tried for robbery
and other crimes. He pleaded Not Guilty, and
attempted to prove an *alibi*. The evidence of
M'Farquhar *alias* M'Rory, as to the facts before
detailed, and Alexander's identity, was positive; and other witnesses were adduced on the
part of the crown to corroborate, by circum-
stantial evidence, the testimony of the principal
witness. Mackintosh produced several witnesses to prove that it was not he who fired at
M'Rory, and that he never in his life accompanied Edward in his lawless pursuits—his
habits being quiet, peaceful, and honest. Some
of these witnesses had been acquainted with
Edward and his associates, and their evidence
was therefore in a great degree disregarded.
His counsel made an able and eloquent appeal
in his behalf; but the charge of the judge—
who, in summing up, told the jury that very
little reliance was to be placed on the credibi-
lity of the witnesses for the defence—entirely removed the impression which the prisoner's counsel had made ; and from the positive testimony

* At Inverness Spring Circuit 1773.

of M'Rory, and the bad notoriety which the prisoner's brother, Edward, and his companions had acquired, the jury, after some deliberation, returned a verdict of *Guilty*. The prisoner heard the verdict with the same calm and decent composure which he manifested throughout the trial. The court was crowded to suffocation, and great sympathy was manifested by the majority of the audience for the prisoner, whom they believed to be innocent, and none felt and sympathised more than the present narrator of these events. The most death-like silence pervaded the Court—every countenance reflected the awful solemnity which all felt, and, in slow and impressive language, the Judge pronounced the dreadful sentence of the law—the most awful it can inflict — death. Even during the delivery of this terrible judgment—every word of which sunk into the prisoner's soul, and called forth tears of compassion and pity from many not used to the melting mood—even in this dreadful hour the prisoner flinched not—no weakness such as might have been expected on such an occasion manifested itself, and his fine handsome form, clad in the humble gray *thickset*, or homespun corded cloth, stood erect and firm, with the dignity so characteristic of the Highlanders on great and solemn occasions. Not a limb trembled—his look was sad, but steady, and not a muscle moved, except a slight quivering of the lip,—immoveable as a rock. Neither terrified nor dismayed by the awful scene around

he appeared the impersonation of manly forti-
tude and conscious innocence, bearing calamity
without shrinking. When the Judge had
ceased, Mackintosh, fixing his eyes steadily on
him, solemnly and emphatically denied his
guilt ; and said, that although he had been
guilty of many sins against his Maker, for which
he hoped for forgiveness, he called that God
before whom he must soon appear, to witness
that he was as innocent of the crime for which
he was condemned as the infant at the breast.
This declaration, at so serious a moment, and
with a certain and ignominious death before
him, produced a strong impression on the
audience, which was increased by pity and
commiseration for his wife and family. His
wife was a mild and gentle creature, and in
every respect, a most amiable woman. The
prisoner was removed from the bar amidst the
prayers and blessings, both loud and deep, of
the greater portion of the audience.

At length the day of Mackintosh's execution
arrived. How solemn was that dreadful day !
Such as could leave their avocations did so in
the morning, and paraded the streets in gloomy
silence, or, if they spoke, it was only in whispers.
By twelve o'clock the streets were almost entirely deserted, and nearly half the population
of the town and neighbourhood was collected
round the gibbet. It was erected at Muirfield,
a little above the town, upon the top of the hill,

> " ———, from whose fair brow,
> The bursting prospect spreads around."

and on which several splendid villas have recently been built. It was then, however, bare and naked—its desolate and cheerless appearance suiting well to the appalling scene that was about to take place. The day was cold and cloudy. The spectators ranged around, looked with anxious fear on the unconscious instruments of death. At length the culprit, accompanied by two clergymen (the Rev. Messrs Fraser and Mackenzie*), the magistrates, and a strong *posse* of constables, appeared. Mackintosh ascended the fatal ladder with a steady and firm step, and stared vacantly around—he appeared overwhelmed by internal agony—his face was pale, and large drops of perspiration rolled down his cheeks. The Rev. Murdo Mackenzie almost immediately commenced to discharge his sad duty. He began by prayer, to which the prisoner listened with the utmost attention, and his countenance became more settled, as if communing with his Maker and composing his soul. After prayer a psalm was sung, the voices of the assembled multitude raising in solemn consonance into the air. Methought, says John, the very wind wafted the heart-giving offering to the Throne on high. Mr Fraser thereafter read a text, and commented upon it at considerable length,

---

* The Rev. Alexander Fraser was minister of the *second charge* at this time ; he died 12th January 1778.

The Rev. Murdoch Mackenzie was at the date of this trial minister of the *first charge;* he died 7th April 1774.

The subject of discourse was the great merit of the Redeemer's blood; and, as he proceeded, with great earnestness and animation, he consoled, cherished, and elevated the culprit's soul by expatiating on the goodness and infinite mercy of God, and the efficiency as well as the universality of the Redeemer's sacrifice, and the divine again concluded by praying, in so earnest and pathetic a manner as to draw tears from young and old. All eyes were now rivetted on the person of the unfortunate victim. The executioner slowly adjusted the noose and pulled down the white cap over his face. The feeling of the crowd was intense—no one breathed—a load oppressed all,—the brain became giddy, and every faculty, physical and mental, seemed convulsed when the culprit's voice broke in accents of piercing agony upon the ear, and sunk into the heart—the last words he uttered were—" Oh, Father, Son, and Holy Ghost, I come." The sound was still murmur ing in the breeze when the crowd were startled by a short, sharp knock, or jerk—a something falling, but not distinctly seen, that

" ——— strikes an awe
And terror on the aching sight,"

and the culprit's lifeless body was swinging in the wind, and his soul winging its flight into the mansions of eternity. With mingled feelings of sorrow and horror, the multitude slowly and silently dispersed, many, if not most of the company, placing a small piece of bread under a stone, which, according to a superstitious tradi-

tion, would prevent after-dreams of the unfortunate Alexander Mackintosh.

After hanging the time required by law, the
body was cut down, and according to the sentence, was placed in an iron cage, which was
suspended from the top of a post near the
gibbet, in order to be a warning and terror, in
time coming, to evildoers. During the afternoon, crowds of persons who had not the courage to be present at the execution, were to be
seen going to view the body in the cage, and
many were the good things said of the deceased.
While the young women, in particular, heaved
a heartfelt sigh for his untimely and dreadful
end, the elders were loud and pathetic in their
expressions of commiseration for his widow and
children, and the old and gray-headed indulged
in groans and ejaculations touching the career
of the family, interspersed with doubts—rather
indicated by a grave shake of the head than expressed—that those who were the condemners
would have an awful account to give of that
day's work. At last night closed in, and hid
with its mantle from the gaze of the curious,
the lifeless body of *Alister Macintosich.*

Notwithstanding the harsh and persevering
attempts of every successive Government—from
the accession of William the Third to the throne
down to the period of which we write—to destroy the feudal power of the chiefs and to extirpate that feeling of clanship which had so
long and so powerfully prevailed amongst the

Highlanders, they still secretly, and sometimes openly, maintained their attachment to their chief, and their friendly and brotherly feeling to their namesakes and clansmen. Neither the Disarming Act nor the defeat at Culloden had extinguished this species of filial feeling between the members of the same clan, and although the law was now too powerful to permit this feeling to display itself on an extensive scale in the open field, still it manifested itself not unfrequently at fairs and district gatherings— sometimes at marriages and funerals—and at times in the everyday business of ordinary life. The clan Mackintosh, in particular, had preserved with the utmost tenacity that spirit of clanship; and the disgrace which the execution of even an illegitimate member of the clan was supposed to bring upon the whole, was sensitively and painfully felt by them, and yet though they knew the fruitlessness of any attempt to impede or obstruct the course of justice, a few of them, resident in and about the town of Inverness, came to the determination of preventing any long continuance of the exposure of the body by cutting it down and interring it. Amongst the number was William Mackintosh, a dyer, better known by the name of " Muckle Willie the Dyster," who from his daring and great strength was looked upon as a leader. The day, as we have said, had been cold and cloudy, and towards evening showers of drizzling rain began to fall, the wind gradually increased, and about seven o'clock, when the dyer and his companions thought it safe to put their purpose into execution, it swept along in strong gusts   The night was very dark—not a star was to be seen—and as the Mackintoshes stole cautiously out of the town, they, in an undertone congratulated each other that the night was so favourable for their design.   They walked circumspectly and slowly until they reached the burn of Aultnaskiach, when they proceeded up the bed of the burn until they arrived at the bridge which crosses it, beyond the late Provost Robertson's house. From that place they crept, rather than walked, over the barren heath, in the direction of the gallows.   The eager dyer, in the exuberant ardour of his feelings for the honour of the clan, urged upon his companions (some of whom he perceived to be faint-hearted) to be firm and resolute, and stand by him; telling them that the honour of the clan was at stake, and that not a moment was to be lost.   They did not, however, much relish Willie's proposition and appeal, but insisted on the necessity of caution. Whilst the ardent dyer was thus endeavouring to convince his associates, the whole party (with the exception of the dyer) were almost transfixed with fear, by hearing a short, hard, screeching sound at no great distance from them.   The clansmen stood statue-stiff—each held his breath—every one listened attentively to catch the faintest sound—every eye was strained to penetrate the darkness of the night, to discover the cause of the interruption —every heart beat with fear and apprehension, and a cold clammy sweat trickled down their cheeks. For upwards of a minute, the whole party stood fixed and mute—nothing was to be seen—nothing heard, save the whistling of the wind and the grating sound produced by the swinging of the iron cage wherein the body was suspended. The party, however, seeing it like a black cloud hanging in the horizon above their heads, became irresolute and discouraged, and were on the eve of returning home, when Willie broke the silence by a very unceremonious " Pooh, you heard nothing but the wind. If there was any noise, why did I not hear it too ? Come, come, let us do our work, and the —— tak' the hindmost." On this they feebly and slowly followed Willie, who sprang to the post, and climbing up with the agility of a cat, was speedily sitting on the top undoing the fastenings, and in a few minutes the cage, with its contents, fell at the feet of his companions with a crash, which they afterwards solemnly declared shook the earth under them. The body was taken out of the cage with the utmost despatch, and carried across the moor to the bank of the burn. Here they made a hole in the sand with their hands, in which the body was deposited, and covering it over, returned to their dwellings, inwardly congratulating themselves that so disagreeable and dangerous a piece of business was ended,

and resolved never again to be engaged in
such an enterprise under any circumstances
whatever. In the morning, when it was discovered that the body of Alister Mackintosh had
been taken away during the night, a reward
of five pounds was immediately offered to any
person who should discover the perpetrators of
this daring act, and considerable excitement was
created in the town by the circumstance. Towards evening, a claimant appeared in the person
of Little Tibbie, the wife of Archy the water-
man. She had been at Aultnaskiach burn for
sand, and to her amazement discovered the
stolen body of Mackintosh. She, with great speed
repaired to the town to claim the reward, and,
burning with the importance of her discovery
and anticipated reward, roared out as she ran—
" Oh, sirs, sirs, Saunders Mackintosh's body! "
She proceeded to the house of the Provost, who
himself was a clansman ; but a faithful clansman,
who had heard Tibbie proclaiming the discovery
she had made, arrived at the residence of the Provost before her, and communicated the disagreeable tidings that Saunders' body had been found.*

* The finding of the body caused the Provost displeasure, and no wonder, as Alexander Mackintosh was
his cousin in the third and fourth degree, as under :—

LACHLAN.	2ND	BORLUM.	
1			2
William, 3rd Borlum.			John.
William, 4th Borlum.			Angus.
1		2	
Lachlan, 5th Borlum.	Shaw, 6th Borlum.		Phineas, Provost, 1773.
1		2	
Edward, 7th Borlum.	Alex., half-brother of Edward, 1773.		

The Provost, although obliged in the discharge of his duty to offer the reward, was by no means sorry that body of his namesake had been taken down, and there were some who even insinuated that he was the instigator of the act himself. Be that, however, as it may ; when Tibbie made her appearance before the Provost, she was not only coldly received, and the promised reward flatly refused, but she was likely to have more kicks than halfpence ; for she was threatened with a night's lodging in the blackhole. In the meantime another party of the clan, headed by the ever ready dyer, proceeded with the greatest expedition to Aultnaskiach burn and removed the body to Campfield, where it was again interred, and allowed to remain.

The narrator relates the singular occurrence of a descendant of the Borlum family, whose life had been forfeited to the law, being buried not many yards from the spot where Provost Junor was assassinated more than two centuries before, and he does not fail to ascribe to the Great Ruler of Events the circumstance which thus so forcibly realised the truth of the commandment, that " The sins of the fathers shall be visited upon the children to the third and fourth generation." Standing upon this spot, and recalling to memory the former pride, power, and cruelty of the Mackintoshes of Borlum — their subsequent misfortunes and disgrace—how variable appear the vicissitudes of human affairs, and the danger and instability of human greatness, and over the grave of the unfortunate Alister, how appropriate would be the line,

"Proud lineage ! now how little thou appearest."

The widow and children of Alister were amply provided for in every respect by the humane and patriotic Bailie Inglis, a gentleman who was continually

"Doing good by stealth,
And blushed to find it fame."

The eldest son, James, entered the Gordon Fencibles, and was speedily promoted, but soon thereafter died.   He was a truly worthy young man.   Edward, the second son, entered the navy, but the Inverness historian never heard what his ultimate fate was.   There was also a daughter, who, after being educated in all the branches of education suitable to a lady of rank, repaired to the south.   She was an amiable girl, and much respected by all the genty of the town and neighbourhood.

That Alister Mackintosh was innocent, was very generally believed at the trial, but the subsequent fate of M'Rory increased and confirmed the suspicion.   The latter very rapidly sunk in general estimation.   His respectability and supposed wealth quickly left him, until at last he became a solitary outcast—in the midst of society, stamped with the brands of perjury and murder—and a few years after the execution of poor Alister he terminated his miserable existence in the village of Beauly.

The estate of Raitts subsequently became the property of James Macpherson, Esq., the celebrated translator of the poems of Ossian, who changed its name from Raitts to Belleville—the original name being in his, as well as in the estimation of others, obnoxious. This property he highly cultivated and improved, whereon he built an excellent mansion-house.

SIMON LORD LOVAT.

THERE are few men who figure more in the history of the stirring times in which he lived than Simon Fraser, Lord Lovat; and there is none who took an active and prominent part in public affairs, and was a principal actor in the plots and counter-plots which were projected or carried into execution in those times, whose actions are so variously represented, and whose motives are so difficult to be ascertained and accounted for. He has himself left an account of his actions, and assigned motives for his conduct, which are contradicted by historians who were contemporaneous with him ; and subsequent historians, more diligent and more impartial than their predecessors, while they have not been able satisfactorily to dispel the uncertainty with which his history is surrounded, have been all but unanimous in impugning the truth of his own version of his conduct, and in portraying him as a man who had exerted considerable talents for bad and selfish purposes. To fathom the depths of such a character, and to lay open motives which preceding historians have been unable to penetrate, are not the objects of the present sketch ; and all that an old man, who is neither versed in the mysteries of character or the learning of schools or histories proposes to do is to communicate to others those scraps of information which he has picked up in his youth from those who saw and knew Lord Lovat well, in the hope that they may amuse others, and perhaps cast a feeble ray of light on one of the most intricate characters in history.

Simon Lord Lovat was born in the year 1663.* He received an excellent education, of the advantages of which he fully availed himself in after-life. In his youth—that period which stamps the future man—he was thought ful and reserved, evincing, however, great forbearance, if not amiability of disposition ; and possessing a complete control over his temper and passions, and exhibiting a shrewd, penetrating, and quick mind. After his boyhood had ripened into manhood, and he had succeeded to the management of the family property, he was a kind, sympathising, and enterprising landlord. On his own estates he was much beloved, and by his friends and neighbours respected and esteemed.

The first act which brought him prominently before the public and involved him in the meshes of the law, was an alleged rape on the Dowager

---

* John Hill Burton states that Simon Lord Lovat was born about the year 1676. He follows Lovat's own statements at his trial and the inscription put on his coffin.

Lady Lovat, sister of the Duke of Athole, who was as distinguished for her benevolence as for her exalted rank.* We say for an alleged rape, because Lord Lovat himself, in his Memoirs, distinctly denies that he was guilty of any such crime, and he appeals with considerable truth in corroboration of his innocence to the fact, that after he had been so charged, he was much beloved, respected by all persons in his own immediate neighbourhood, who had the best means of making themselves acquainted with the facts. Be this, however, as it may (for it is surrounded, like most of his actions with doubt), it is certain that criminal proceedings were instituted against him, and that as he had failed to appear, a sentence of outlawry was pronounced against him, to avoid which, and the vengeance of the Duke of Athole, he fled to France.† It is equally certain (for the author had the story from those who were personally

* There was a forced marriage with the sister of the Duke of Atholl, and the ceremony was performed twice, first at Castle-Downie by Mr Robert Munro, minister of Abertarff; and to satisfy her ladyship's scruples as to the legality of the first ceremony, a little later on the marriage was re-enacted at Eilean-Aigas, by William Fraser, minister of Kilmorack. The marriage was, however, at the instance of the Atholl family, annulled. Her ladyship lived till the year 1743, and thus saw her whilom husband twice married. Had a few short years more been given to her, she might have witnessed her lord receive the reward of his treacherous conduct.

† Sentence passed on 4th Sept. 1698—condemned to be executed, and his name, fame, memory, and honours to be extinct.

cognisant of the fact), that in order to disgrace
the lady and insult the Duke of Athole, he sent
her home to her brother, riding on a one-eyed
horse, which was led by a one-eyed lad. To revenge so ignominious a treatment, a numerous
band of Athole men, exasperated at the disgrace of the lady, and the insult shown to the
house of their proprietor and chief, marched
northward to attack the Frasers. The wily
Lord having, however, received information of
their approach, fled from Beaufort Castle, and
concealed himself in the rocks behind Clachnaharry. For fourteen days he lurked amongst
the rocks, enduring the greatest possible priva-
tions, and dependent entirely upon the scanty
and precarious bounty of an attached butcher of
the name of John Bain, who resided at Knock-
nagur, close by. Meanwhile the Athole men,
after searching Beaufort and the neighbourhood, demolished a portion of the Castle, and
after a fruitless hunt in quest of the fugitive
through the Aird, were obliged to return home
disappointed. On the retirement of his pursuers, Lord Lovat availed himself of the first
convenient opportunity and fled to France.*

On his arrival in France, Lord Lovat presented himself at the Court of St Germains, but
James, the exiled King, who had heard of the
charge brought against him, refused to receive
him, and debarred him from appearing at

* In 1702.

Court.* In consequence of this repulse, it is said that he entered into holy orders, and for some time had charge of a nunnery. It is not unreasonable to suppose that while thus occupied (an occupation by the way not very suitable for a person who had been guilty, or at least charged with rape, under very cruel and aggravating circumstances), Lord Lovat became thoroughly initiated in the principles of the Jesuits—principles which throughout the rest of his life he practised with so much ability and so little scruple.

While occupied in a watchful and pious superintendence of the nuns, Lord Lovat had a correspondence with several leading men in his native country, and among others with the Duke of Queensberry, who is said to have invited Lord Lovat from France to conduct a conspiracy, which had for its object to bring the Dukes of Hamilton and Athole, and other courtiers who were obnoxious to the Duke of Queensberry and the Duke of Argyle into disrepute with Queen Anne, who had just ascended the throne.

---

* His offer to aid the cause of King James was suspected. He, however, received a commission from Louis XIV. in 1703 to visit Scotland and test the feelings of the Jacobites towards the exiled family at St Germains, but one or two secret agents were despatched to watch his movements. His mission was a failure, and on his return to France he was accused of trafficking with the British Government—was arrested, and sent to the Bastile, according to some but Lovat (in his own Memoirs) says he was imprisoned in the Castle of Augouleme for three years.

Before he left France he had succeeded in obtaining from the widow of King James a commission of Major-General, and on his arrival in Scotland, he made use of this commission to entrap the enemies of Queensberry and Argyle into a conspiracy against the Government, but not succeeding in his mission so well as he expected he was again sent back to France. Lord Lovat himself, in his Memoirs, gives a very different account of his embassy to Scotland , but it is beyond our sphere to attempt to reconcile the various conflicting accounts of his objects and proceedings. On his return to France, and when the whole conspiracy became known, Lord Lovat was confined in the Bastile * by orders of the French King, for having imposed upon the widow of King James in the matter of the commission of Major-General.

After remaining for some years in restless confinement in France, Lovat at length succeeded in obtaining his release from a French prison, and had the art also to obtain a conditional pardon from the English Sovereign. Before the breaking out of the rebellion of 1715, and when that ill-conceived and worse-conducted outbreak was in embryo Lovat was suspected of being implicated in treasonable practices, and he was apprehended, but by the interposition and indefatigable exertions of a Mr Patrick Nichol-

* It is very questionable if Lord Lovat was ever confined in the Bastile. His first prison was the Castle of Augouleme, and thereafter in banishment at Saumur.

son, who was a chaplain in one of the Royal Regiments, and perhaps from the absence of conclusive evidence, he was acquitted. After his acquittal he all at once became a zealous partizan of the existing Government, and used all his art and talent to obtain credit and influence with the leaders of the Whig party.

Lord Lovat now all at once became a zealous partizan of the Government—having collected a large body of his own clansmen (the Frasers), and assisted by no inconsiderable body of the Grants and other neighbouring clans, he determined on capturing the fort of Inverness, then in the hands of the Chevalier's friends, under the command of Sir John Mackenzie. This determination, which required both courage and prudence, he planned with his usual tact and ability. Having formed his plans with great secresy and dexterity, he attempted to surprise the Castle, but in this he was defeated. Capt. Rose, who had charge of the detachment that was to lead the assault, was repulsed at all points. Again and again, he led his kinsmen to scale the walls, but was gallantly repulsed by the Governor. The town and the neighbouring country was in the possession of Lovat, and knowing that the Castle could not long hold out, he prudently resolved not to waste his men and ammunition in fruitless attempts to take a castle by force which he knew its defenders must soon yield of their own accord, he therefore ceased in his attempts to take the Castle by force. Sir

John Mackenzie availed himself of the earliest opportunity afforded him either by the negligence or the design of the besiegers to abandon the Castle and escape across the Ferry into Ross-shire. Lovat of course immediately took possession of the Castle, an event which was at the time of the greatest possible importance to the Government, and which very materially contributed to the complete defeat of the Chevalier and his friends, which almost immediately followed.

The Government could not well overlook the claims of an adherent who had rendered such important service at so critical a moment ; and besides other favours which he received, Lord Lovat was entrusted with a very extensive command in the north. Borlum Castle, Brahan Castle, Erchless Castle, and the lands and residences of several other distinguished and gallant chiefs were in his hands or under his vigilant watchfulness, and for a time he exercised the authority of a local Lieutenant Governor over a considerable part of Inverness and Ross-shires.

But the restless, the intriguing and the unsatisfied spirit of Lord Lovat, would not permit him to remain at ease. Either because he conceived himself not sufficiently rewarded by the Government for the services which he had rendered, or because he anticipated from the success of the cause of the Stuarts greater benefits ; or, what is not unlikely, because " the neb of him could never be out of mischief," he was one of the first who engaged in and concocted the rising of 1745. In the October of that year, a meeting of those friendly to the cause of Prince Charles, was called by Lord Lovat, at which a great number of persons attended, and on that and on several previous and subsequent occasions, he not only used all his influence, but all his policy and powers of persuasion, to induce his dependents and neighbours to join him in taking arms against the Government. While he was thus secretly exerting himself in the cause of the Prince, he was not altogether idle with respect to that of the Government. He was even at this time in correspondence with President Forbes, and to him he made the most violent protestations of attachment to the Government; and so artfully and plausibly did he conduct himself, that he succeeded for a considerable time in imposing on the worthy President. Even when his clansmen were in arms, and marching towards Edinburgh to join the forces of the Prince, he still continued to assure the President that he was firmly attached to the Government, and that his clansmen had marched contrary to his orders at the instigation of his son, whose actions he found it impossible to control.

When the Frasers were in the field, Lord Lovat, who was too infirm too sustain the fatigues of a campaign, was hatching treason in the north—keeping a fair face to both parties. After the retreat of the Highlanders from Eng-

land, it was, however, a point of importance to
secure " the old fox," and with this view Lord
Loudon and President Forbes approached his
" burrow," and by specious speeches prevailed
upon him to proceed with them from his residence to Inverness.   He was required to bring
all the arms of his clan by a given day, which
he promised to do ; but failing to perform his
promise, sentries were placed at the door of the
house in which he lived, and he was virtually a
prisoner. But the old adage, that " old birds
are not to be caught with chaff," proved good
on this occasion.   For old Lovat, suspecting
the intentions of Loudon and President Forbes,
gave them leg bail by escaping by the back
door.   The slip which Lord Lovat gave his
keepers occasioned them great inconvenience
and disconcerted their plans, and no doubt
protracted the final fall of the Stuart hopes.

After the battle of Culloden, Lord Lovat was
obliged to leave his own part of the country,
and take refuge in a small island in Loch
Morar, where, it is said, he had been compelled
to subsist for several days on meal and water,
and where he was apprehended in the month
of June 1746, having concealed himself in the
hollow of a tree.   He was immediately conveyed to London, where he arrived in August.
He was impeached before the House of Peers
in December, and his trial commenced on the
9th of March 1747.   The trial continued for
several days, and throughout Lord Lovat con-

ducted himself with uncommon skill—but the facts were too glaring—he was unanimously found guilty, and doomed to death. On the 9th of April 1747, rather better than one hundred years since, this most extraordinary man was beheaded on Tower Hill, London, and during his trial, imprisonment, and execution, his conduct was firm and dignified.* May his body

* There has been always a question as to where Lord Lovat's body was buried. His own desire was that it should rest in the north among his own clansmen, and to this request the Government assented ; but Horace Walpole and others assert that the permission was rescinded, and the body buried in the Tower. The following interesting letter, for which we are indebted to Colonel A. J. Warrand of Rye-field, sets another light on the matter. The writer, Hugh Inglis, was of the Kingsmills family. He sailed his own vessel " The Pledger " between Inverness and London ; we meet his name frequently among documents of this period. Bailie Gilbert Gordon, to whom the letter is addressed was a merchant, and for many years a member of Council and Town Treasurer :—

" My dr Sir,—I wrote you by last post, and now as then, can give you but poor encouragement with regard to our fishing. Never poor people were so unlucky as to the sale ; still large quantities arrive daily. Rob. Rodger is not yet come up. What has happened in his adventures is still a mystery to me, tho' there will be no difficulty in recovering the insurance I hope.

" Poor Lord Lovat was beheaded a few hours after writing you my last. He behaved like ane old true duelnach,† quite undaunted even to the last ; made several witty speeches, which seemed quite agreeable to the bulk of the people. His corpse is to be brought down by ' The Pledger.'

" I have been looking out for ane sloop, but none to be had worth the buying. I expect to be loaded this ensuing week, and if our old good luck is with us, I hope to be with you soon. Very best wishes to good Mrs Gordon and all true friends.—1 am, my dear sir, yours for ever,   " Hugh Inglis."

"London, 11 Apl. 1747.
" Mr Gilbert Gordon, mercht., Inverness."

† Duelnach—*Diùlnach*—a hero.

rest in peace, and may his soul inhabit the mansions of bliss! Let posterity imitate his virtues and avoid his errors!

The life of so extraordinary a character is replete with anecdotes, and one or two of these we shall lay before our readers. We have already said that a Mr Nicholson, a Presbyterian minister, had used great exertions to get Lord Lovat out of the meshes of the law on the eve of the outbreak of 1715. For this generous and disinterested act, Lord Lovat presented him to the united parishes of Glenconvinth and Kiltarlity.* This was the first Presbyterian minister settled there—the incumbents of Glenconvinth and Kiltarlity for twenty-eight years previous being Episcopalians. The first day he went to preach, he took a sword and target with him — Lord Lovat accompanied him. They expected strong opposition, and it is true a large *posse* of females made up their minds to offer resistance ; among these was honest Peggy Bain, a relative of the narrator's. With aprons tied round their waists, well filled with stones, the fair Amazons were determined, when the worthy minister should come out of the church, to maltreat him ; but his preaching had such effect upon them, that whenever they came out, they skulked behind the wall of the burying-

* The Rev. Patrick Nicolson was ordained to the parish of Kiltarlity 16th July 1716, died on 7th March 1771, his successor being his youngest son, Malcolm Nicolson.

ground, and there deposited their *grape*. Some years after, Mr Nicholson so far carried on the discipline of the Kirk as to order, of course not for good conduct, Lord Lovat on the " cutty stool." This order sadly militated against the pride and wishes of his lordship. Being, however, assured by his friend, Mr Fraser, town-clerk of Inverness * (whom he consulted in the matter), that the law of the Kirk was imperative, and that nothing but compliance would save him from excommunication, he consented to the punishment, upon a promise from the worthy Town-Clerk that he would stand by him for three Sundays in the church of Kiltarlity. Mr Nicholson, who was then the John Knox of the Highlands, being about to address the lordly occupant of the " cutty stool," Lord Lovat exclaimed, " Ah, Nicholson, you ungrateful man, was it not I that placed you there ? " (having presented him to the living), whereupon Mr Nicholson answered, " True, my lord, you have placed me here, and I have placed you there to-day to be publicly rebuked for your sins." Lord Lovat, however, thereafter forsook the church of Kiltarlity, and became a hearer of Mr Chisholm of Kilmorack.

Of Lord Lovat it was remarked by some that there was not a single good act in his life ; but the compiler of these sketches says : " Did he

* William Fraser of Bught, writer, and Town-Clerk of Inverness. He was familiarly known in Inverness as " Clerk " Fraser.

not place the Rev. Messrs Nicholson in Kiltarlity, Chisholm in Kilmorack, and Thomson in Kirkhill,* than whom, in their day, Scotland could not produce three greater divines." Looking back to a period of some years after the affair of the Duke of Athole's daughter, Lord Lovat on one occasion sending his principal servant, Donald Cameron, on an important mission to Glenmorriston, gave him a shilling to defray the expenses of the journey. Donald indignantly looked at the coin and his noble master, and said in Gaelic, " Do you think, man, lord (he never addressed him ' my lord '), that a shilling would bring me back and forward between this and Glenmorriston ? " On this his lordship said, " Tell whose servant you are, and you will not want on the way." " I tell you, man, lord," said Donald hastily, " that if I would tell whose servant I am, every one between this and Glenmorriston, would shut the door upon me." His lordship replied, " O, Donald, Donald, if you knew how many a hard and trying hour I suffered before now, whilst lying hid amongst the black stones of Clachnaharry, you would not complain of a shilling being too little to bring you between this and Glenmorriston.

Lord Lovat had an only brother, the Hon. John Fraser, who was obliged to fly the country

* The Rev. Robert Thomson from Clyne, Sutherlandshire, admitted to Kirkhill 22nd April 1717, died 30th April 1770 in the 85th year of his age.

to evade the punishment which would most likely overtake the tragic event of which he was the author. Accompanied by a few youthful spirits of the clan, he attended a market in the village of Beauly. The amusements of the fair they enjoyed very well, and as they were returning they heard the sounds of the bagpipes issuing from a barn, where a party of Highlanders were dancing to its shrill notes. Listening for some time to the tune, the peculiarity of which first attracted their musical organs—one of the young men remarked it was played in contempt of Mr Fraser, and that if it were he who was alluded to, he would instantly put it beyond the power of the piper to play any more that evening. This remark roused John's spirit to such an angry height, that unsheathing his dagger, he entered the barn determined only on ripping up the bag of the pipes. His sudden appearance in the barn, with a dagger glistening in his hand, as if courting provocation, and rage depicted on his countenance, and the applicability, in that attitude, of the words of the song to him at that moment, certainly drew on him the scornful looks of the dancers. The piper, the unfortunate object of his rage, sat, unconcious of the fuel he was adding to the flame, at every note he struck of "Ha bitac air Mhac Thomais," &c. Mr Fraser, inflamed at what he conceived an insult, quick as thought plunged his dagger to the handle in the heart of the poor piper, who instantly dropped down dead. Mr Fraser, with his evil advisers, immediately fled from the barn—remorse adding swiftness to his flight. Finding that Beaufort Castle was no secure retreat for him from the minions of justice, by whom he was pursued during that and the succeeding two days and nights, he hid himself within the sea mark at a place called Morich. This was within a few miles of the noble mansion in which he was born and brought up. At times he covered himself with the sea weed, affording but a very uncomfortable bed and hiding-place for one of his breeding; but he was forced to submit to anything for security. From this cold and insecure place of concealment he contrived to reach the house of a faithful clansman in Stratherrick, by whom he was most kindly received. With this attached adherent he remained for some time in perfect security, until his brother, Lord Lovat, furnished him with a sum of money to carry him out of the country,—which he left soon thereafter.* The melancholy affair threw a gloom over the whole tenantry on the extensive estates of Lovat, and the sympathy of the north generally was excited in behalf of Mr Fraser. Many supposed that had he stood his trial he would have been acquitted, in consequence of its not being a premeditated act, but solely

---

* The disappearance of this brother of Lord Lovat's, and whose fate has never been ascertained with certainty, has led to the many claimants from time to time to the estates of Lovat.

arising out of the unceasing provocation, and at the wicked instigations of his companions. The tune " Ha bitac air Mhac Thomais," which was the occasion of the perpetration of the murder, is a very old one, and was originally composed out of contempt to one of the lairds of Applecross. Although Mr Fraser's dress exactly corresponded with its words, yet the poor piper had not the least intention of offending any person when he was playing it ; besides, the family Gaelic name of Lovat is "*Mhac Shemie,*" while that of Applecross is "*Mhac Thomais.*" So that the only allusion it could bear to the Hon. John Fraser was that his father's name was Thomas, and it was merely this which led his companions to infer that it was played in derision. The tune is still in repute, and an excellent one too ; but it is wrong to suppose, as some do, that it was the murder of the piper which originated it—it was long before then well known.

Lord Lovat left two sons, the Hon. Simon Fraser,* Master of Lovat, and Archibald. The

---

* Simon Lord Lovat left three sons—(1) Simon, Master of Lovat, by his first wife, Margaret Grant, fourth daughter of Ludovick Grant of Grant, born 1726, and was thus nineteen years of age when concerned in the Rebellion. (2) Alexander, born in 1729, died in 1762, unmarried.

Lord Lovat, by his second wife, sister of the Duke of Argyle, had one son, (3) the Hon. Archibald Campbell Fraser. The latter, after many years passed in the public service, resided in the neighbourhood of Inverness. Many stories are told of his eccentricities; but he had also many

Master was but a youth about seventeen when the patrimonial estates were forfeited. He had joined in the rebellion at the instigation of his father, and was too young to be a guilty participator in it, and he was therefore a fit object for the mercy of the Crown. Through the exertions and influence of the Duke of Argyle and his friends a commission was procured for him in the army. His chivalrous and brave military career more than realised the encomiums passed upon him by his Grace of Argyle, and the assurances he had given the Government of Mr Fraser's loyalty. He distinguished himself greatly in the first American war, where his gallant conduct soon attracted the notice of his superior officers, and the commander-in-chief wrote home of the gallant daring of Colonel Fraser at the taking of Quebec. Intelligence of this. and of the probability of his being speedily installed into the inheritance of his forefathers, arriving, the Aird and other Lovat estates were all in one blaze with bonfires, and in Inverness the demonstrations of rejoicing were equally great—bonfires and firing of guns were the order of the day. The inns were filled, and the quaich and coggie successively went round. At a party of these glad spirits the author had the honour of acting as croupier. In a large procession, headed by a piper, he acted also a conspicuous part. The procession

good qualities, and was a gentleman of great public spirit. He died in 1815.

received a great augmentation and decidedly handsome appearance from a number of females joining, and especially those of the clan Fraser, on observing which the author ran home for his aged mother, she being a Fraser, who, when informed of the event, was right glad and joyful to join the happy cavalcade.*

Subsequently Colonel Fraser arrived as Major-General, and entered into full and uninterrupted possession of the estates. He was afterwards elected Member of Parliament for Inverness-shire.† The Government not being

---

* In 1772 Colonel Fraser was rewarded for his distinguished service to the Crown with a free grant of his family estates forfeited in 1746.

† Elected M.P. in 1761. He had meditated standing for the county representation in 1754, as appears from the following letter addressed to a clansman. We are indebted for the copy of it to T. R. Biscoe, Esq. of Newton :—

Letter addressed to Hugh Fraser, younger of Dunballoch. To the care of Angus Mackintosh of Drummond, Inverness.

"DEAR SIR,—The friendship you expressed when I was in the country, and the desire to serve me demands that you should know the state of my affairs at present. Prudential considerations have made me resolve to lay aside thoughts of standing for the county of Inverness at this time, and as that is the case I wish all my friends wou'd appear and vote for Mr Campbell, younger of Calder.* I don't know if you have been long enough infeft, but if you have I hope you will go in and vote.

"It wou'd be too tedious to mention in a letter the particulars that have made me come to this resolution; when we meet you shall know it all. Meantime I think myself as much obliged to you as if I had occasion for your vote, and am as much convinced of your good disposition towards me. Pray remember in the kindest manner to all at Newton, and believe me, dr sir, your most obedt. humble servt.   "S. FRASER."

"London, Aprile 23rd, 1754.

---

* Pryse Campbell, yr. of Calder, elected 1754, sat till 1761.

tired of his valuable services, conferred a higher command upon him. He raised the 71st Regiment of Highlanders, and was on the eve of again embarking for America, when he was suddenly taken ill and died in England.* He was succeeded in command by Lord Balcarras. It may well be said that General Fraser's actions more than doubly atoned for the iniquities of the father. His brother, Archibald Fraser, also a firm and loyal friend to the House of Hanover, succeeded him in the paternal possessions, and subsequently the present noble proprietor.

In concluding these sketches, we cannot help calling attention to what will no doubt suggest itself to every reader,—the contrast of the Lord Lovat of 1747 and the Lord Lovat of 1847.† The former, as already observed, was proud, crafty, and avaricious—the present, amiable, kind, and generous, and easy of access to the lowest individual on his estates, and one who wishes the well-being of every one on his extensive domains. He is also one of the most liberal and kind landlords known, while the great delight of his noble lady‡ is to be constantly doing good—feeding the poor, clothing

---

* Died in 1782.

† Thomas Alexander Fraser.

‡ Charlotte Georgina Jerningham, daughter of Lord Stafford.

the naked, and to their children extending the blessings of education. Long may they live to enjoy their exalted rank and extensive estates and to bear the thanks and blessings of the poor !

LORD PRESIDENT FORBES.

FEW names occupy a more prominent or dis-
distinguished place in the annals of Scotland than that of Lord President Forbes ;
and in the eventful era in which he lived he
stands pre-eminently distinguished in the history of the times, as one of whom it would be
difficult to decide whether his public or his
private virtues preponderated, or exercised the
greater influence over his actions. In whatever
light his conduct is viewed, whether as a man,
a Christian, or a patriot, we are struck with the
consonance—the uniformity and the consistent
harmony of his life, in thought, principle, and
action, in all the multifarious and frequently
conflicting circumstances which influenced and
sometimes controlled his conduct. It is difficult to say whether simplicity, integrity, or
benevolence were the most prominent charac-
teristics of his mind. His patriotism was
deeply tinged with benevolence, his political
character was marked by the strictest moral integrity, and his most comprehensive plans as a
statesman (and his were the only comprehen-

sive plans of and for the time) are no less to be admired for their simplicity than their ability and wisdom.

Amidst the heterogeneous mass of mercenary sycophants, corrupted parasites, and sincere patriots, who supported the Government, or swelled the ranks of those interested, discontented, or mistaken hosts that thronged round the standard of the Stuarts, there is not one man who took a principal part in the stirring events of that period, whose motives are so pure and praiseworthy, whose conduct is so blameless, or who conferred on his country a tithe of the benefits which resulted from the prudence and wisdom of President Forbes. While he was devoting his best energies to secure the throne and consolidate the Government, he was no less laborious to save the chiefs and clans who sided with Prince Charles, and were doing all they could to overthrow the Government. Like Blanche in the play of King John, he seemed to think that he had a divided duty, and to say—

> "Which is the side that I must go withal?
> I am with both : each army hath a hand;
> And in their rage, I having hold of both,
> They whirl asunder and dismember me."

Firmly attached to the Government, he sincerely wished it success, and yet afraid of the terrible fate which would await the friends of the Prince in the event of defeat, he could not contemplate the success of the Government but with a feeling of horror. Ordinary minds would have sunk under such conflicting feelings, but the very necessity which called for the most constant watchfulness, and intrepidity on the part of the President, appeared to give him renewed will and power for the discharge of the duties which his position in the Government, and his attachment to his friends, would seem to have imposed on him.

Of such a man it would indeed be presumptuous in the humble narrator of a few disjointed facts connected with the Forbeses of Culloden, to attempt any biographical sketch , and it would be still more unpardonable to attempt to give an analysis of the qualities and conduct of President Forbes. In the foregoing observations we have only endeavoured to give expression to the feelings and opinions with which the President was regarded in and about Inverness during his lifetime, and by those who knew him best,—who had good opportunity, from their intimacy with himself and from their knowledge of his conduct and their personal acquaintance, with the circumstances in which he was so prominent a performer, of forming a just estimate of his merits.

Before we proceed to narrate those traditional and historical facts with which we became acquainted in our youth, concerning the President, we think it right to lay before our readers a short account of the history of his ancestors from the time at which they settled in Inverness-shire.

Duncan Forbes, or *Dunachac na Boiceannan*, the first of the family of Forbes, who came to Inverness-shire, and who was the founder of the family, was the eldest son of Mr John Forbes of Badenley, second son of Alexander, laird of Tolquhoun.* Mr John Forbes having died young, leaving a wife and three children (Duncan being the eldest), the widow was induced to entrust Duncan to the care of a gentleman who became tutor to Lovat, and who was married to Duncan's aunt, and Duncan accompanied them to their residence, Beaufort Castle, about the year 1569. He was then sixteen years of age. His aunt and her husband paid every attention to his health and education, and both prospered under their fostering care. At the age of 20, Duncan Forbes had few superiors in the Highlands for strength, agility, and intelligence. And in 1594, having, as was the prevailing practice of the age, betaken himself to "the use of arms," he distinguished himself at

---

* About 1567, John Forbes of Badenley married Elizabeth Keith of Tulloes, and had by her Duncan, first of Culloden, etc. Duncan Forbes of Culloden, eldest son of John Forbes, married Janet Forbes of Corsindae, by whom he had John Forbes of Culloden and other two sons and two daughters. John Forbes of Culloden married Anna Dunbar, only daughter of Dunbar of Grange, and by the said Anna had Duncan Forbes of Culloden and other five sons and two daughters. Duncan married Mary Innes, daughter of Sir Robert Innes of that Ilk, and by her had two sons, John and Duncan—this latter the Lord President Duncan Forbes—and seven daughters.

the battle of Glenlivet, where he exhibited surprising courage, and had the honour of assisting
the Earl of Argyle and his (Duncan's) relative
Lord Forbes in the cause of the King against
the Lords Huntly and Erroll.

He very shortly thereafter bade farewell to
the profession of arms, and was by his step-
uncle employed in a more peaceful but more
intricate business, viz., in examining and adjust-
ing certain accounts and family matters, at
which he made but slow, or at all events, but
unprofitable progress. The consequence was
that he left the business entrusted to him by
his step-uncle, and took up his residence in Inverness, where he commenced business as a
skin merchant.

Being of an amiable, affable, and humane
disposition, he gained the esteem and good
wishes of those who had the pleasure of coming
in contact with him, and as his friendship was
becoming more extensive and firm with his
fellowmen, his business was the more rapidly
prospering. His country residence was Drakies,
now known as Ashtown, the property of Æneas
Mackintosh, Esq. of Raigmore. Speaking of
the estate of Raigmore, comparing it eighty
years ago with what it is now a strange contrast
is perceptible ; then it was mostly a cold, barren,
and bleak moor—now it is one of the most
beautiful and fertile properties in the country,
adorned by an elegant mansion-house, and surrounded with shrubberies and plantations. A

short distance from Raigmore House there is a small pond, of which a few swans and geese keep possession in mutual fellowship. These improvements were principally made by the late proprietor, and show how sterile wastes can be converted into most fruitful fields. Below the house where it now stands, ran the uncontrollable burn, Alt Mourniack, reputed as the rendezvous of witches, and which no travel- ler, after nightfall, had the hardihood to pass ; but now a good Parliamentary road renders it safe at all hours of the night. To return to Mr Forbes, or as he was more familiarly known in Gaelic as *Dunachac na Boiceannan.* Mr Forbes on one occasion invited a party of gentlemen to dinner at Drakies, and requested his lady to prepare a good dinner for them. At the ap- pointed hour the guests arrived—among them was Cuthbert of Castlehill and his son ; but Mrs Forbes, either from penurious motives, or from having no great regard for some of the party, prepared nothing more than the ordinary family dinner, which hurt the feelings of her husband so much, that as on former occasions when he was likewise very much provoked, he determined for a time to " cut her acquaint- ance." The morning following that on which the dinner party took place, Mr Forbes rose very early, as if going to town ; but to town he did not proceed. Night came on, but he did not return to his own fireside—the next morn- ing came and still there was no appearance of the absent husband. Mrs Forbes became greatly alarmed for his safety, and accused herself of having offended an affectionate husband, and would now give worlds, if she had them at disposal, to have him back again. Weeks, months, and even years rolled on, but they brought no tidings of the worthy burgess who had so precipitately disappeared from the arms of a loving wife and a large circle of admiring and attached friends and acquaintances.

At length, however, Mr Forbes was discovered in the Western Isles, pursuing his business more extensively than before, purchasing all sorts of skins—shipping them to Liverpool and other ports in England. In the Hebrides he continued for some years, but having gone to London to settle affairs with some merchants, he purchased a vessel, which he loaded with all sorts of fancy goods, and sailed for Inverness. The vessel being noticed from the town at the mouth of the river Ness, the majority of the population ran down to see the largest vessel that ever entered the river. Among the spectators was Mrs Forbes ; and as the ship neared the quay, she noticed her long lost husband standing beside the captain at the helm. In an instant she gave a scream of joy, and fainting, fell into the arms of a lady who accompanied her. Mr Forbes well knew the voice, and quickly leaping ashore amidst the plaudits of the people, clasped his senseless wife to his bosom. She soon rallied, but her sudden joy

threatened to be too much for her to bear. The
joyful demonstrations of the people were beyond
description. He now commenced business still
more extensively as a general merchant and
shipowner, being the only one at the time in the
northern metropolis. Taking a walk one summer evening with his lady, they strolled out in
the direction of Culloden, then belonging to
The Mackintosh. When they reached Culloden, the masons were after laying the foundation stone of the Castle. Mr Forbes gave the
men a shilling (no small sum in those days) to
drink, but Mrs Forbes demurred a little to this
piece of extravagance, to which her husband replied, "Who knows, my dear, but you and I
may be the occupants of this Castle, and possessors of Culloden." Six months had scarcely
elapsed from the time when this conversation
took place when Mr Forbes was possessor of
Culloden. That took place in 1624.* Only
one storey of the Castle was then above the
ground, when Mr Forbes completed it. On
the lintel above the main door, were The Mackintosh's initials, and part of the armorial bearings, which were never defaced. In the year
1625, Mr Forbes built a splendid edifice as a
town house in Church Street, which was pulled
down in 1810. In 1626 he became chief
magistrate of Inverness a situation which he
filled for several years with credit to himself

* The barony of Culloden was purchased from the laird
of Mackintosh in 1626.

and benefit to the town and its inhabitants. In 1654, having been thirty years in possession of the estate of Culloden, he was gathered to his kindred at the age of 82, much regretted by all who knew him. His likeness is still to be seen in a state of good preservation at Culloden House. In the Chapelyard, Inverness, over his tomb and that of his lady, are the following lines :—

> " These polished stones
> Placed here above thy bones
> Add to thy honour not a whit
> Which was before, and still remains, complete,
> Thy memory shall ever recent be
> Preserved by such as draw their blood from thee,
> Who in regard of thy good fame,
> Receive reward by claiming to thy name ;
> For thy remains do honour to this place,
> And thy true virtue honours all thy race."

Duncan Forbes was succeeded by his eldest son John, who, from the treasures left him by his father, was enabled to purchase the barony of Ferrintosh, which afterwards became so celebrated for the distillation of whisky, although for many years not a single drop has been made on that property. He subsequently (in the year 1670) purchased the property of Bunchrew,* a favourite resort of the great President.

---

* Bunchrew. A small property about three miles to the north-west of Inverness. In 1843 it was sold, and purchased by the late John Fraser, a native of Inverness, and is still in possession of his family.

John was succeeded by his son Duncan, who was a very amiable man, and who, like his father, was a pious and exemplary man. He again was succeeded by John, the fourth laird, who was a very active patriot. He sat for some years in Parliament,* where he frequently distinguished himself for his patriotism and his advocacy of his countrymen. He died in 1734, and was succeeded by his brother Duncan, then Lord Advocate.

Duncan Forbes, the most eminent Scottish patriot and statesman of his time, and as a statesman, perhaps the most distinguished that the country has ever produced, was born in the year 1685, in a small, unpretending, but not uncomfortable house close to the seaside on the estate of Bunchrew,† about three miles to the west of Inverness,—a retreat interesting not only on account of its being the birthplace of this truly great man, but also, and still more interesting, as the favourite retreat to which he withdrew in his secessions from severe labour to mature fresh plans for the benefit of his country.

Having completed his studies at home he made a tour to the Continent, visiting and making some stay in those towns renowned for

† He represented Nairnshire from 1704-7, and again 1713-15 ; Inverness-shire 1715-22 ; and Nairnshire a third time 1722-27.

† Born at Bunchrew 10th November 1685.

learning,* where, no doubt, he overlooked nothing of interest to the scholar, and gained information which proved of the greatest utility afterwards.

Mr Forbes, on his return from the Continent, applied himself to the study of the law. He resided for some time with his uncle, Sir David Forbes of Newhall, Mid-Lothian, who was an eminent lawyer. In due time he was admitted a member of the Faculty of Advocates,† and had subsequently the office of Lord Advocate conferred upon him ; and he also represented the Inverness District of Burghs in Parliament.‡ Of his Parliamentary conduct it is not our province to speak at length ; but there are one or two points connected with it which we feel called upon to notice. In 1725, we find Mr Forbes, then Lord Advocate, introducing a bill for disarming the Highlanders. Strange to say, some of the clauses of the bill were rejected, or rather dropped, in consequence of the opposition of the *English* members, and Lord Advocate Forbes's attempt at legislation, while it proved distasteful to the Highlanders, was opposed by the English squires. The bill, although harsh in appearance, was in reality the best course that the Government could have pursued. It

* He studied, after the manner of Scottish students in those days, at Leyden for one year.
 † He passed at the Scottish Bar in 1708.
 ‡ He sat as member for the Inverness burghs from 1722 to 1734.

is gratifying to observe that even in the Parliament of 1725, while the work of corruption was
at its height, that a majority of the English
members, entertaining more extended notions
on, and having a better appreciation of, the principles of liberty as secured by the Constitution,
resisted parts of the bill of Mr Forbes the Lord
Advocate, himself a Scotchman and a Highlander. But while we cannot help expressing
our admiration of the motives which influenced
the opponents of the bill we are bound to say
that no better measure could have been suggested for the purpose of preventing any rising
in the Highlands. The provisions of the bill
were applied in our own time in principle, for
successive years, in the Irish Arms' bill, and
without entering into political discussion on the
justice or harshness of that measure, we may
remark that in applying it to the Highlands of
Scotland, inhabited by a purely military people,
immediately after they had taken arms against
the Government, and at a time when the people
of the country made little secret of their desire
to see the Government overturned, the same
principle which was resorted to one hundred
years afterwards, and with all the advantage of
the experience of that period in the case of Ireland, proves at all events, if not the wisdom or
the justice of Lord Advocate Forbes's bill in
1725, that he is entitled to the credit of the
plan, and that as regards Scotland it was subsequently successfully carried out.

Mr Forbes, during the whole of his Parliamentary career, was not only consulted by the Government, but was, in fact, the chief law officer of the Crown in Scotland, and also the representative of the interests of the whole kingdom, in Parliament, as well as his Majesty's advocate for his Majesty's interest. Mr Forbes having risen to the highest position at the bar was elevated to the bench. His talents and knowledge of the law as well as his patriotism, were soon rewarded with the highest judicial appointment recognised in Scotland—Lord President of the Court of Session ;—and the next measure with which we find his name associated is, the scheme for raising the independent Highland companies. This was in 1739. As the measure to which we have before referred was intended to deprive the Highlanders of the power of doing mischief to themselves or the Government, that to which we now advert had for its object to confer upon them the power of doing good, both to the Government and to themselves. This plan, although it was at the time when it was first proposed rejected, was eventually carried out, and the benefits which it conferred on the Highlands, were not only largely felt at the time, but are participated in at this moment by thousands of the descendants of gallant soldiers who availed themselves of the honourable employment thrown open to them by the Goverment.

The most interesting feature to the public in the character of this noble-minded and highly-gifted man, was the judicious and patriotic part he acted in the eventful and stirring rebellion of 1745-46. Hearing that Prince Charles Stuart landed on the west coast of Inverness-shire, and that several chiefs, with their clansmen, were mustering and enrolling themselves under his banner, he cast his official wig aside, and hastened down to Culloden to warn his tenantry and friends of the portending, and prevent their enlisting in the Pretender's ranks. The Prince's claim to the throne, the means at his command to make good the same, the futility of these, and the consequences to the country, he impartially laid before the Government and the clans ; in consequence of which, together with his powerful influence and assiduity, it is allowed that fully ten thousand men were dissuaded from taking up arms in behalf of Charles. So heartily attached was the President to the House of Hanover, that he raised, clothed, and paid out of his own private means a regiment of fine men, for which he received no compensation whatever, and which had the effect further of greatly embarrassing the family for some time.

The President, when arrived at Culloden, instantly had the Castle fortified, and he himself was busily employed, day and night, writing despatches to different parts of the country ; and wherever the Pretender happened to be, he was sure of finding that President Forbes had been there before him with his letters, causing the people to keep quiet and not join with him.

Charles was, of course, aware of the sway exercised by the President over the people, and was
not a little chagrined at the success attending it.
But of all the chiefs who embraced his cause
none was more enraged at the President than
my Lord Lovat, for which it was well known he
entertained private and selfish motives. First,
he expected, in the event of Charles Edward
bringing the enterprise in which he was engaged to a successful termination, a dukedom
would be conferred upon him; and secondly,
that the picturesque estate of Bunchrew, the
property of the President, but originally that of
the Frasers, would be added to his other
estates in the Aird. Illustrative of the feeling
entertained by Lord Lovat towards President
Forbes, it may be noticed, that on each side of
the road at Bunchrew grew some large black-
thorn bushes, overtopped here and there with
alder trees, proving an eyesore to his lordship
as he passed to and from Inverness, and the
great agricultural improvements which were
made on the estate likewise added fuel to the
flame already burning within him, so that when
he entered Inverness, the first person he was
sure of calling upon was the amiable Provost
Fraser, who would generally inquire of his lordship—" What news from the Aird ?" " Nothing,
but that the black thorns of Bunchrew stab me
to the very heart's core every time I pass."
President Forbes likewise planted those portions
of Bunchrew not adapted to agriculture with

trees, some of which can still be seen towering majestically above the mansion-house.

Bunchrew was the spot, during vacation time, which the worthy President delighted to frequent, and where he always resided. His great partiality for this beautiful locality must have been owing to its being his birthplace, and the pleasure and delight he experienced in improving and ornamenting it must be ascribed to the same cause. At Bunchrew, likewise, he further delighted to receive and entertain many of the more highly respectable visitors who came to the neighbourhood, who were quite enchanted with the President's affable manners and the decorations of his estate. Some of them mentioning so to Lord Lovat, galled the latter not a little, while few, if any, visited him at Beaufort Castle save his friend the chief of Macleod.

The President, sojourning at Bunchrew on one occasion, where he often kept convivial parties, invited the Town Council of Inverness to dinner. The deacon of the weavers, on sitting down to dine with his brother councillors, began to show the extent of his knowledge and appreciation of modern discoveries and refinements by calling for a dish of tea, just then as great a delicacy as could be named in the house of the Highland laird. Hospitality, however, placed everything within command at the service of the guest, although it was out of the regular order. A domestic having prepared and brought in the tea, with a valuable set of china, placed the beverage on a side table, the deacon being invited to move to it to partake of the tea. The dinner table groaned under a load of substantial Highland cheer, and the civic functionary, intent on that which was immediately before him, so far forgot the cap of gentility he had assumed as to break out into a violent passion, declaring it an insult to request him to take refreshment at a table separate from his companions.* During this paroxysm of rage, he commenced laying about him in wild Highland style, demolishing the valuable service of china in a very brief space of time. The President, instead of imitating the rage of his guest, passed over the damage and misbehaviour by humorously saying, "Well, well, deacon, it cannot be helped; I will make the shuttle pay for it some day," alluding to the offender's craft. This mild reproof, while it formed a striking contrast to the weaver, was in keeping with the high character for personal and domestic worth and piety for which the

* It is curious, in connection with this story of the worthy deacon and his tea, to note that the President, while in Parliament, had entered on a crusade against the use of "the cup that cheers." Instead of this article, which has changed the entire social habits of the country, he proposed to substitute ale, and he bewails the miseries that would follow the disuse of malt when working men took to the use of tea in place of their accustomed drink, and working women to the use of the same drug instead of the usual "twopenny."

President was so justly celebrated. The members of the Council, on leaving the ever-hospitable house of Bunchrew, were each presented with a hat, some of whom up to that time never had a hat on their heads. So important a present was then only worn on state occasions, being at other times carefully laid by in the "muckle kist;" and the deacon alluded to was, in his latter days, the first and only tradesman in Inverness who began to wear a hat every day, and the novelty was so great that crowds followed him wherever he went. At times it was with difficulty he kept them at a respectful distance when he took up his evening station on the "old bridge" to contemplate the beauties of the scenery around his native town. The honest deacon at last had to give vent to the displeasure he felt at the conduct of his admirers, whom he reproved by saying, "What do you see about me, sirs? am I not a mortal man like yourselves?" These reproofs had often to be administered, and being generally in the same words, the expression "Am I not a mortal man like yourself," became a cant phrase in the town and neighbourhood for many years afterwards.

But to return to the "troubles" of the '45. After a course of uncertainty, the laird of Macleod at length became a firm supporter of the Goverment in consequence of the persuasion of the Lord President. Frequent communications took place between them. Macleod's valet was kept constantly on the road with despatches between himself and the Lord President. The valet had come in contact on his journey with some of Prince's followers, and for fear of being searched by them to discover what his frequent missions were, he always carried a large staff, with a hole, so artfully and neatly executed as to defy the closest scrutiny. In this cavity was deposited the letter ; and the Dunvegan " gillie maol " passed and repassed the rebel parties without detection.

It having come to the knowledge of President Forbes that Lord Lovat was secretly engaged in forwarding the interests of Prince Charles, he immediately despatched a messenger with a remonstrance, warning him of his danger, but to his friendly advice his lordship replied he took no part whatever, but believed his stiff-necked son had. The Master of Lovat a few days afterwards hearing of this, told his hoary-headed parent in tears, " I'll go myself to the President and tell him the whole truth ; " but the fears of the youth were soon calmed when his father told him that Prince Charles would be triumphant, and that then he would be raised to the dignity of a Duke. To the young amiable Earl of Cromertie, to whom he was particularly attached, the President was also sending friendly advices, which Lord Lovat understanding, he on his part was sending him his trusty and confidential servant, Donald Cameron, urging him to be firm in the Prince's cause, and heed not the delusive advices of either the President or the Rev. Mr Porteous.

The President's indefatigable exertions in support of the dynasty of the House of Hanover were now so well known, and the success generally attending these, that the wrath of the rebels against him became so fierce and deadly that several plots were devised to cut him off, but few were found hardy enough to carry these into execution. However, Mr John Fraser of Ericht, in the parish of Dores, Inverness-shire, even though a staunch Presbyterian, and notwithstanding the urgent remonstrances of his father-in-law, the good and pious Mr Chisholm, first Presbyterian minister of Kilmorack, and his own parish clergyman, the worthy Mr Bannatyne of Dores,* was so thoroughly bound up in the Prince's cause, that all arguments to dissuade him proved of no avail. Mr Fraser held the rank of captain in the rebel army; and about ten days previous to the battle of Culloden, Captain Fraser, heading a party of his clan, all bound by oath that they would neither eat nor drink until they had taken President Forbes dead or alive, marched at midnight to Culloden Castle to take it by surprise and seize the President; but on nearing the Castle they were observed by a sentinel stationed on one of the turrets, who gave the alarm, and the assailants

* The Rev. Archibald Bannatyne from Ardchattan, admitted 14th September 1731, died 20th June 1752.

were received with a fearful discharge of shot, which wounded many but killed none. Captain Fraser and his lawless band quickly retreated. He escaped unhurt, as he likewise did on Culloden Moor, which sealed the claims of the Prince, and brought ruin on those of his adherent, who escaped the bloody day. One of these was Ericht, with whom the narrator was intimately acquainted ; and many a time have they sat down together to relate the events of Ericht's life, mourning over the wreck of his home, and the loss of his beautiful little estate, and the blindness which reduced him from affluence to penury, and expressing sorrowful compunctions for neglecting the sound counsels of his dearest friends and relatives. Ericht was one of the most handsome Highlanders ever seen, and when in his better days a guard of honour consisting of twelve men in full Highland costume escorted him to and from the kirk. When the gallant and brave General Simon Fraser, after the taking of Quebec, where he highly distinguished himself, returned to his native country, to resume possession of his patrimonial estates, forfeited by his father, whose treasonable conduct he more than atoned for, hearing that Ericht was still living and very poor, sent for him and offered to procure him a commission in the army, but this he refused. Poor Ericht, reduced from independence, now to the greatest poverty, and when his locks were grey, went to Perth, and there as a private soldier, enlisted in the Grant's regiment.

Another gentleman, who had the good fortune when the rebellion was in its infancy, to receive a pressing invitation from President Forbes to spend a few days with him at Culloden, was Sir Alexander Macdonald of Sleat, in Skye. The President was led to believe that Sir Alexander, with his clan, contemplated joining the rebels on his [the Prince's] landing in Skye, and being well aware of the sway he exercised in these places, as well as his anxiety for him as a friend, had therefore sent for him to prove the utter fallacy of the claims of the Pretender, and the ruin consequent on the attempt, and, happily for Sir Alexander, he returned home convinced, after spending a few agreeable days with the worthy President. The flag of rebellion was unfurled in the Isles; but it found Sir Alexander firm at his post. The result being already well known, it is needless here to repeat it. Suffice it to say that Charles Edward Stuart, accompanied by the faithful Flora Macdonald, compelled to relinquish his aspiriug views, was a refugee, with a price set upon his head, and after many hairbreadth escapes, eluded the pursuit of his enemies, at last reached Skye, and with Sir Alexander Macdonald's knowledge, was at one time concealed within a mile of his house at Monkstad, where at the time he was entertaining a party of royalist officers.

> "War tests the magnanimity of man,
> Sweet the humanity that spares a fallen foe."

Sir Alexander, though he knew the very spot

where the Prince lay hid, and the easy certainty
with which he could be captured, despised be-
traying him into the power of his enemies.
Many true and faithful Highlanders acted a like
noble part.

After the battle of Culloden, President
Forbes exerted all his influence and ingenuity
to save the lives and property of those who had
taken up arms against the Government, but his
efforts were not always successful. The fiendish thirst for blood evinced by the Duke of
Cumberland could not be satiated,—the prisoners, the wounded, and the dying were
butchered without mercy, and in the ranks of
the conquering army the only cry was "kill,
kill." The President again and again raised
his voice against the massacre, and entreated
the victors to "spare," but the work of death
still went on, and the ministers of vengeance
heard not his voice. Even in his own house
the work of destruction went forward. After
the battle, eighteen wounded officers, unable to
join in the flight of their companions, secreted
themselves in a plantation near Culloden Castle.
They were however, discovered, brought to the
Castle, where they were kept for two days in a
room under ground, in a state of the utmost
torture, without receiving medical or other aid
except such as was afforded by the kindness of the
President's steward. They were then huddled
into carts, carried out of the courtyard, ranged

in a row against the wall, and shot to death.*
The destroying fiends proceeded in their work.

* A statement by John Fraser, an officer in the Master of
Lovat's Regiment, was published, in which he relates the
cruel barbarity of this fact, of which he himself was the
sole survivor. Some hours after the defeat of the Highland army, he, with seventeen other wounded officers of
that army (who were either carried or made their escape
towards a little plantation of wood near to the place where
Fraser lay), were carried to the close and office-houses of
Culloden, where they remained for two days, wallowing in
their blood and in great torture, without any aid from a
doctor or surgeon, though otherwise kindly entertained by
Mr. Thomas Stewart, chamberlain and chief housekeeper to
the late Lord President; and this he did to some at the
hazard of his life. The third day, Fraser and the other
seventeen wounded officers were, by a party of soldiers
under the command of a certain officer, put on carts, tied
with ropes, and carried a little distance from the house to the
park-dike, and there planted against the wall or park-dike,
when the officer who commanded the party ordered Fraser,
and the other prisoners to prepare for death, and all
who were able bended their knees and began to pray to
God for mercy to their souls. In a minute the soldiers who
conducted them were ordered to fire, which they did, and
being at the distance only of two yards from the breasts of
the unhappy prisoners, most of them all expired in an instant; but such was the humanity of the commanding
officer as thinking it right to put an end to so many miserable lives, that he gave orders to the soldiers to club their
muskets and dash out the brains of such of them as they
observed with life, which accordingly they did. One of
the soldiers observing Fraser to have signs of life after receiving a shot, he struck him on the face with the butt of
his musket, broke the upper part of his nose and cheekbone
and dashed out one of his eyes, and left him for dead. A
certain young nobleman, riding out by the house of Culloden and the park-dike, observed some life in Fraser, and,

Mr Hossack, the Provost, who had, under the President, performed good service to the Government, was induced to apply to the Duke of Cumberland to entreat him to stay his destroying hand. The Duke was attended by Generals Hawley and Huske, who were deliberating with him as to the speediest mode of putting his prisoners to death at one fell swoop. The Provost said, "As his Majesty's troops have happily been successful against the rebels, I hope your excellencies will be so good as to mingle mercy with judgment." Hawley in a rage cried out, "D—n the puppy, does he presume to dictate here? carry him away!" An officer in attendance offered to kick Hossack out, and the order was obeyed.* The Provost of Inverness, a firm and

calling out to him, asked him who he was; he told him he was an officer in the Master of Lovat's Regiment. This young lord offered him money, saying he had been acquainted with his colonel; upon which Fraser said he had no use for money, but begged for God's sake either to cause his servant to put an end to his miserable life, or carry him to a cot-house, which he mentioned, at a little distance. This the young lord had the humanity to do, and Fraser being put into a corn "kilnlogie," where he remained for three months, and with the assistance of his landlord was so far cured as to be able to step upon two crutches.

* We append the following more particular account of this incident :—

"Provost Hossack, with the magistrates, having gone to the levee to pay their compliments, hearing orders were given to shut the ports that no rebel might escape, and that the meeting house should be burned and the man who preached in it, said he hoped they would mix mercy with judgment, upon which they said, 'D—n you, puppy! do

useful friend of the Government, was kicked
down stairs by a servile hireling, because he
pleaded for mercy! Oh, Glencoe! Oh, Culloden! The God of justice and of battles
will yet avenge thee!

On his return from Skye, the President himself went to the Duke, and with that firmness
and candour which distinguished him, he stated
to the Duke that the wholesale slaughter that
was going forward, was not only inhuman and
against the laws of God, but contrary to the
law of the land, which he called upon his Royal
Highness to observe. But what said the Duke
to the man, of all others, to whom the House
of Hanover, was most indebted? " The laws
of the country, my Lord!" said the Duke with
a sneer, "I'll make a brigade give laws, by
God." Shortly afterwards he visited London
and being asked by the King if the reports in
circulation of the atrocities committed by the
Duke of Cumberland were true, he answered,
" I wish to God that I could consistently with
truth assure your Majesty that such reports
are destitute of foundation." The King abruptly

you pretend to dictate here?' They ordered him to be
kicked down stairs; accordingly he was tossed to the stair
head from one to another, and there one of a considerable
character [Sir Robert Adair] gave him a toss that he never
touched the stair until he was at the foot of the first flat of
it. These gentlemen were ill-rewarded, for none could be
more attached to the Government than they were; but they
had compassion on the distressed and oppressed, which was
then an unpardonable crime of the deepest dye."

and in displeasure left him—his accounts
with the Government were with difficulty
passed, an immense balance was left unpaid,
the House of Hanover had discharged its debt
of gratitude, and President Forbes was heard of
no more ! ! !

But it is painful to dwell on this subject. It
is difficult to say which excites most surprise,
the cruelties of Cumberland, or the ingratitude
of the King and the Govermeut. But what is
even still more surprising is, that in more peaceful and juster times, the claims of the Culloden
family should have been forgotten by successive
Governments, and that the possessors of the
Crown have not remembered to whom in a
great measure they owe it.

As a Christian, President Forbes was a man
who truly ruled his own house. Morning and
evening a bell was rung for worship, and none
were permitted to absent themselves on any
pretext. The narrator recollects seeing a small
volume entitled *The Life of Faith*, which had
formed part of the President's library, and the
margin of every page of which was covered
with his criticisms. His public character was a
most upright and exemplary one—his private
one nothing less ; he was beloved and happy in
his family—esteemed by his domestics and dependants, and surrounded by attached relatives
and friends and acquaintances, and worn with
over study and care, this amiable and distinguished individual was, in the year 1747, and at

the age of sixty-two, like a clock worn out with eating time," gathered to his fathers. His name and fame will live for generations yet to come. He was succeeded by his son John, likewise a most exemplary man.

The beetling stone, which supplied the place of a mangle, on which Mrs Urquhart, the President's washerwoman, used to dress his linens, is still in the narrator's possession. This stone was bequeathed as a legacy by Mrs Urquhart to his mother, then the principal washerwoman in Inverness.

The Culloden family from the first were eminent for their loyalty, and in the person of the present amiable young laird the virtues of his ancestors are reflected.

SIR GEORGE MACKENZIE OF ROSEHAUGH.

MANY, no doubt, have read in the pages of history of the celebrated Sir George Mackenzie of Rosehaugh, one of the most talented members of the Scottish bar, who, in the reign of Charles II. was Lord Advocate of Scotland, and whose Institutes are still considered as standing authority by the legal profession. Of him the author says, that on one occasion while at Rosehaugh, a poor widow from a neighbouring estate called to consult him regarding her being repeatedly warned to remove from a small croft which she held under a lease of several years; but as some had yet to run before its expiry, and she being threatened with summary ejection from the croft, she went to solicit his advice. Having examined the tenor of her lease, Sir George informed her that it contained a flaw, which, in case of opposition, would render her success extremely doubtful; and although it was certainly an oppressive act to deprive her of her croft, he thought her best plan was to succumb. However, seeing the distressed state of mind in which the poor woman was on hearing his opinion, he desired her to call upon him the following day, when he would consider her case more carefully. His clerk, who always slept in the same room with his lordship, was not a little surprised, about midnight, to discover him rise from his bed fast asleep, light a candle which stood on his table, then draw in his chair and commence writing very busily, as if he had been all the time wide awake. The clerk saw how he was employed, "but ne'er a word he spak'," and, when he had finished, saw him place what he had written in his private desk, then lock it, extinguish the candle, and retire to bed. Next morning, at breakfast, Sir George remarked that he had had a very strange dream about the poor widow's affair, which, if he now could remember, he had no doubt about making out a clear case in her favour. His clerk rose from the table, and requested from him the key of his desk, brought therefrom a good many pages of manuscript, and as he handed them to Sir George inquired, " Is that like your dream ?" On looking over it for a few seconds, Sir George said, " Dear me, this is singular ; this is my very dream ! " He was no less surprised when his clerk informed him of the manner in which he had acted, and sending for the widow, he told her what steps to adopt to frustrate the efforts of her oppresssors. Acting on the counsel thus given, the poor widow was successful, and, with her young family, was allowed to remain in possession of her " wee bit croftie " without molestation.

Sir George principally resided in Edinburgh, and previous to dining invariably walked for half an hour. The place he selected for this was Leith Walk, then almost a solitary place. One day in taking his accustomed exercise, he was met by a venerable looking, gray-headed gentleman, who accosted him without either introduction or apology—" There is a very im portant case to come on in London fourteen days hence, at which your presence will be required. It is a case of heirship to a very extensive estate in the neighbourhood of London, and a pretended claimant is doing his utmost to disinherit the real heir, on the ground of his inability to produce proper titles thereto. It is necessary that you be there on the day mentioned ; and in one of the attics of the mansion-house on the estate, there is an old oak chest with two bottoms ; between these you will find the necessary titles, written on parchment." With this he disappeared, leaving Sir George quite bewildered ; but, resuming his walk, he soon recovered his former equanimity, and thought nothing further of the matter. While taking his walk the second day, he was again met in the same place by the old gentleman, who earnestly urged him not to lose another day in repairing to London, and assured him that he would be handsomely compensated for his trouble ; but to this Sir George paid no great attention. The third day he was again met by the same hoary-headed gentleman, who energetically pleaded with him not to lose a day in setting out, otherwise the case would be lost. The singular deportment of the gentleman, and his anxiety that Sir George should be present at the discussion of the case in which the old man seemed so deeply interested, induced him to comply with his importunities, and accordingly started the following morning on horseback, and arrived in London on the morning preceding that on which the case was to come on. A few hours saw him in front of the mansion-house described by the old gentleman at Leith Walk, where he met two gentlemen engaged in earnest conversation—one of the claimants to the property and a celebrated London barrister—to whom he immediately introduced himself as the principal law officer of the Crown for Scotland. The barrister, no doubt, supposing that Sir George was come to take the " bread out of his mouth," spoke to him rather surly and disrespectfully of his country; to which the latter answered, " that, lame and ignorant as his ' learned friend ' took the Scotch to be, yet in law, as well as in other respects, they would effect what would defy him and all his London clique." This disagreeable dialogue was put an end to by the other gentleman taking Sir George into the house. After sitting and conversing for a few minutes, Sir George expressed a wish to be shown over the house. The drawing-room was hung all round with beautiful paintings and drawings, which Sir George greatly admired; but there was one, however, which attracted his attention ; and after examining it very minutely, he with a surprised couutenance, inquired of his conductor whose picture that was ? when he was told, " It is my great-great-grandfather's." " My goodness," exclaimed Sir George, " the very man who spoke to me three times in Leith Walk, and at whose urgent request I came here ! " Sir George, at his own request, was then conducted to the attics, in one of which there was a large mass of old papers, which they turned up without discovering anything to assist them in prosecuting the claim to the heirship. However, as they were about giving up their search in that attic, Sir George noticed an old trunk lying in a corner, but was told that for many years it it was placed there as lumber, and contained nothing. The Leith Walk gentleman's information recurring to his memory, he went and gave the old moth-eaten trunk as hearty a kick as he would wish to have been felt by his " learned friend" the barrister. The kick sent the bottom out of the trunk, also a quantity of chaff, among which the original titles to the property were discovered. Next day Sir George entered the Court just as the case was about to come on, and addressed the pretended claimant's counsel with " Well, sir, what will I give you to abandon this action ? " " No sum, or any consideration whatever, would induce me to give it up," was the answer. " Well, sir," said Sir George, at the same time drawing out his snuff-horn and taking a pinch, "I will not even hazard a pinch on it." The case having been called, Sir George, in answer to the pretended claimant's counsel, in an eloquent speech, addressed the bench, exposing most clearly the means adopted to deprive his client of his birthright, and concluded by producing the titles mentioned, which all at once decided the case in favour of his client. The decision being announced, Sir George took the young heir's arm, and, bowing to his "learned friend" the barrister, remarked, "You see now what a Scotchman has done, and I must tell you that I wish a countryman anything but a London barrister." Sir George immediately returned to Edinburgh, well paid for his trouble, but he never again in his favourite walk, encountered the gray-headed gentleman.

THE FAMILY OF CHISHOLM, ETC.

THE Chisholm family is amongst the oldest and most respectable in the Highlands. Their chief residence is Erchless Castle, which is one of the few castles of the " olden time" now standing in its primitive grandeur. It is situated in a lovely valley, surrounded with the most picturesque and romantic scenery, and the silent but rapid stream of the Glass (which is joined by the Cannich and Farrar), wends its way downwards close to the Castle, to join the sea in the Beauly Firth. The elevated and craggy mountains, which rise, as it were, towering to the skies, on each side of the narrow glen, are truly imposing, and are the admiration of the numerous tourists that journey thither. Prior to the construction of the present ancient family residence, the original seat stood on an elevated spot some distance to the north of where the present one stands—and near to which place the remains of the late chief lie, in a beautiful tomb, which is surrounded with shrubbery and evergreens.

Glenconvinth is one of the most beautiful

and picturesque spots in the Highlands of Scotland. Its name in the Gaelic language is *Gleann-a-conn-ɟhioch*, of which the literal translation is " Glen of the Wild Dog or Wolf." This little glen is surrounded and overtopped by the surrounding hills, and concealed from the view of the tourist until he just enters it, when a valley, " rich with the scents of nature's laboratory," bursts upon his sight, with a fine clear stream meandering through the bottom of it, wending its way until it discharges itself into the Beauly Firth. About half way up the glen, at its northern base, may still be seen the ruins of a church, where people were wont to worship in the " olden time ; " also a spacious burying-ground attached. The church, previous to the Reformation, but subsequent to that eventful period, was united to that of Kiltarlity, and is now denominated the United Parishes of Kiltarlity and Glenconvinth.

The tales associated with Glenconvinth are not a few ; its church, bell, and burying-ground being consecrated, were held in the highest veneration by the people of the place and surrounding country. Connected with this hallowed spot are told the following anecdotes :—

In the dusk of one fine evening, as the merry songsters of the grove were winging their airy way to leafy bowers, a poor widow, returning home from Belladrum mill, leading by a halter a Highland garron with a bag of meal on his back, and when passing the burying-ground, the bag dropped off, which, from its weight, the poor woman was unable to replace on the animal's back. In this trying dilemma, and seeing none to assist, the disconsolate widow gave vent to her sorrow, augmented as it must have been by being beside the place where now in peace reposed the ashes of her departed husband. In the agony of her mind she exclaimed, " Well, well, if he that is lying with his head low here to-night was now living, he would soon put the bag on the horse's back." Scarcely had she pronounced these words, and turning round, to her surprise found that the bag was actually replaced, and then proceeded on her way.

The church bell was also an object of reverence, and whatever truth there may be in the words that " coming events cast their shadows before," it is nevertheless stated that this bell has been known to toll when none was near it, giving a forewarning of the demise of some individual whose remains were soon to mix with those of his kindred. A sturdy Highlander from the confines of Strathglass, possessing a greater share of hardihood and daring than is generally to be met with among his countrymen in interfering with any sacred thing—for we are safe in saying, that Highlanders in particular, are more tenacious of their religious observances, and are remarkable for the superstitious awe in which they hold anything connected with their religion or place of worship, much more so than in any quarter of the kingdom—was base enough to carry off the bell one night and hang it up in an oak tree near his residence. At midnight the offender was alarmed at hearing the shrill tones of the bell, but could not summon up enough of courage to proceed to the oak tree and learn the cause. The following morning the bell had again disappeared, but was found in its former exalted position, in the west gable of the Glenconvinth chapel, and none could state how it got there. The distance to which it was conveyed is full six miles, and is still known as *Craobh a-ghlac*, or " the bell tree." The bell was never more interfered with until the year 1745, when a party of Lord Loudon's men, then stationed in Inverness, having taken a stroll through the Aird, hearing of the veneration in which it was held, and viewing it as a Popish relic, took its tongue away, and otherwise destroyed it, to the no small sorrow of the surrounding peasantry. I well remember seeing this bell in its dilapidated state lying in a corner of the ruins of the church.

Glenconvinth, like other places at one period, was infested with wolves and many an unwary huntsman got dreadfully wounded, or lost his life, in an affray with those ferocious beasts ; but by the frequent visits of the lovers of the chase to the locality, their numbers were gradually diminishing, till at last it was supposed the glen had been ridden of this pest, but the havoc made amongst the sheep in the neighbourhood told but too plainly such was not the case. The glen was then, and for a long period thereafter, overgrown with alder trees and hazel bushes, affording an excellent cover to these denizens of the forest, and here it was discovered a wolf of extraordinary size and ferocity had his lair. This was the last one that could be seen—the terror of the place and the dread of the wayfarer. To kill this formidable scourge, and extirpate thereby the race altogether, the neighbouring gentlemen assembled. Among those who met on this perilous adventure was the Master of Chisholm—a young man not yet arrived at manhood. The party were standing a little to the east of the burying-ground, sharpening their spears on a large stone, when the wolf was espied in the valley a little below where they stood. One of the party volunteered to go down alone and despatch the animal, but he had not gone above half way, when perceiving the size of the enemy he was about to cope with, his courage failed and he turned back. The young Chisholm then requested to be allowed to go down, but although the gentlemen admired the valour of the stripling, they dissuaded him from such a rash step, The youth sharpened his spear, after wringing a reluctant consent from the party, and buckling himself, set off to meet his crouching antagonist. whose howlings and fiery eyeballs, flashing defiance, noways dismayed the brave youth. Our hero, coming up, all the time watching closely

the animal, and as he was in the act of springing, pierced the enraged beast a little below
the neck. So great was the force of the blow,
that his hand nearly followed the course of the
spear. The party, who anxiously waited the
result of the combat, were over-joyed, and loud
in their praise of the gallant youth, when they
discovered him unscathed standing on the car-
case of the wolf. The stone on which they
sharpened their spears, still stands as a lasting
relic of the affray, and although frequent using
has considerably defaced it, may still be
pointed out to the traveller who visits this
lovely spot, and among those whom kindred
associations brought to view this renowned
place and see the stone was the late lamented
amiable and pious chief, brother to the present.
Since the above affair, the wolf's head forms
part of the armorial bearings of the ancient and
respectable family of Chisholm.*

Of another chief of this family, there is the
following amusing anecdote :—He had been for
some years greatly afflicted with pain in his
legs, so much so that he was deprived of the
power of walking, and had to be carried about.
As was customary in those days with chiefs and
lairds, every family kept a fool or jester. One
fine summer evening, the worthy chief was carried to a couch prepared for him in the garden,

* Similar mythological stories are told in the history of
several Highland families. The " Centenarian " here has
substituted a wolf for a wild boar. The boar's head is part
of the family arms.

and seeing his fool there too, called him, in order to keep the flies off his legs, which they were tormenting. The fool carried in his hand a large cudgel, and seeing a swarm of flies resting on his helpless master's legs, aimed a blow at them; but instead of killing myriads, as he expected, he nearly broke the chief's legs, and threw him into a swoon. Supposing he had terminated his master's existence, the fool ran away as fast as he could, and betook himself to the neighbouring wood. Soon after the occurrence, some of the domestics entered the garden, and finding the chief in such a condition, were greatly alarmed; but shortly thereafter rallying, he told them what the fool had done—but he was nowhere to be seen. Conjecturing rightly where he had gone, a search was made; but when on the point of giving it up as fruitless, from the top of a thickly branched tree the fool bawled out—" Ye needna, sirs, for mysel' just got mysel'." Having decoyed him down, and on their way expostulating with him for the injury he had done his indulgent master, he replied—" It was the flies that did it, and not me." But in the end it turned out that the poor fool was the best physician his master ever saw, for the disease in his legs not long thereafter disappeared, and there was not a gentleman in the country had a sounder pair than the Chisholm. He lived to a good old age, and esteemed none of his domestics more than his fool.

The next anecdote of this family, relates to a period when the worthy chief was rather seriously indisposed, and an express was sent for his son, Mr William, who was then practising as a physician in Inverness. He lost no time in repairing to the bedside of his sick father, and remained at Erchless Castle for two or three days, by which time his father was out of danger, and said " Now, William, since I am almost quite well, I do not mean to have your services for nothing, therefore you will tell me what is your charge ? " The doctor replied, " Oh ! father, I do not mean to charge anything." But on the chieftain again saying, he would not take his trouble without being remunerated, answered, " Oh ! then, since you are determined to pay I will only charge what I do other gentlemen." " How much is that ? " " Only £50." " Only £50 !" remarked the Chisholm, " do you charge other gentlemen that sum ? " and being answered in the affirmative, said, " Oh, Willie, Willie ! it is I who put the estate into your hands when I made a doctor of you." So rising, and going to a drawer, took therefrom the £50, which he placed in his son's hand. Dr Chisholm was a gentleman highly esteemed by all classes in Inverness, and subsequently became chief magistrate—an office which he filled for years with honour and integrity.* His lady was grand-aunt to Mr Baillie

* Dr William Chisholm was Provost of Inverness from 1773 to 1776, and re-elected 1779—1782. He survived till 1807.

of Dochfour. In benevolence and sympathy she excelled, and wherever sickness or poverty prevailed, her helping hand was extended to alleviate it. This was beautifully exemplified in the year 1781, better known as " the year of the white pease," in which, throughout the length and breadth of Scotia's soil, its inhabitants experienced the distressing effects of a famine. Among others who sent to the Continent for cargoes of pease was the lady's brother, Mr Alexander Baillie of Dochfour, who, on its arrival in Inverness, directed Mrs Chisholm to distribute a considerable portion of it to the most necessitous in the town—the rest to be disposed of to the best advantage, and it certainly would have brought a handsome profit then, as everybody would give any price for it rather than starve, had not this amiable lady represented to him that the poor could not pay for it, and the rich would be provided for in some other way. He then told her to do with it as she thought best. Persons were now appointed to grant " lines " to the poor, some for a peck or a peck and a half, and one of those who had the honour of granting lines was the narrator himself.

The present Chisholm's father was one of those kind and liberal landlords who lived in the hearts of his tenantry and dependants, cherishing a mutual and good understanding with them, and they in return were directed by his superior counsel and advice. Illicit distillation was carried on then in Strathglass to a great extent, and although he was continually pressing on the people the danger and unlawfulness of smuggling, he could not suppress it. At Excise Courts he often presided, and when an unlucky smuggler was brought before the justices, and in all probability amerciating the unfortunate man in a heavy fine, the Chisholm was known frequently to move the sympathy of his brethren on the bench, and set at large for a mere trifle of a fine.

The great and godly Mr David Chisholm, minister of Kilmorack, was a descendant of the Chisholm family. He was a most powerful, impressing, and convincing divine, and an honoured instrument of doing much good in his day and generation. He was succeeded in the parish by his son, Mr David, also a celebrated divine.

THE MACKENZIES OF REDCASTLE.

THIS branch of the Clan Mackenzie, at one time numerous and powerful, may now be said to be extinct.* In former days when violence, rapine, and war, was the all-absorbing business of men, the Mackenzies of Redcastle occupied the southern part of the county of Ross, and possessed in the firth of Beauly (which bounded their estate on the south) a natural barrier of great importance to protect them from sudden invasion or surprise, commanding a view of an extensive portion of the country of the Frasers and the Mackintoshes, and were well situated to act as the scouts and warders of their clan, to communicate information to their chief and his adherents, and to harrass and delay, if they could not effectually oppose, an invading army. In their capacity as sentinels of the clan, they were distinguished by watchfulness and bravery, and rendered

---

* The estate of Redcastle has passed from the Mackenzies. In 1720 it was sold to Mr Grant of Sheuglie for £25,450. In 1790 Sir William Fettes became the purchaser at over £135,000, but it was sold to the family of the present proprietor, J. E. Baillie of Dochfour, upwards of sixty years ago, at a large reduction on this price. For many descendants of the Mackenzies of Redcastle, see The History of the Mackenzies by Alexander Mackenzie, 1894.

important services to their friends. In times of peace, they were, however, characterised by a spirit of tranquillity, humanity, and benevolence, which was seldom evinced in the turbulent times in which they lived.

The period at which the Mackenzies became proprietors and took possession of the estate of Redcastle, is very remote, and not known to the author. In the year 1590,* Kenneth Mackenzie, then laird of Redcastle, a gentleman of great worth, and endeared to his friends, tenants, and dependants by his amiable and engaging qualities, resided in the family castle at Chapeltown, situated a few hundred yards north of where the present castle stands. From his peaceable and impartial conduct to all with whom he came into contact, he obtained a character for integrity, intelligence, and justice, and the disputes of his more quarrelsome neighbours were referred to his decision. Not only was he esteemed and respected by those lairds and chiefs in his own county and immediate neighbourhood, but his friendship and acquaintance were solicited by many at a distance. He was particularly intimate and a great favourite with the then chief of the Clan Cameron, and on the invitation of the chief, paid frequent visits to the residence of Lochiel in Lochaber.

In the year 1598, the Earl of Huntly, created

---

* According to Mackenzie's history of the clan (1894), Redcastle did not come into the possession of the Mackenzies before 1608.

Marquis in the later part of that year by James VI., went on a hunting excursion to the wilds of Lochaber. The Marquis was a keen sportsman, and devoted much of his time to that noblest of British, or perhaps of any sports, deer stalking, then pursued with an ardour and on a scale of greater extent and danger than in these degenerate days, although of late years something of the spirit and enthusiasm of the olden times seems to be reviving among those who devote themselves to this glorious pursuit. To receive so important a personage as the Marquis of Huntly with suitable respect, and to enable him to follow his favourite amusement on an extended and splendid scale, Lochiel invited to his castle, not only the gentlemen of his own clan, but several lairds and chiefs far and near, and amongst them Kenneth Mackenzie, laird of Redcastle. The sport was carried on for several days with all the ardour, skill, and success of practised sportsmen, and great was the destruction which the numerous party made amongst the antlered monarchs of the braes of Lochaber and the surrounding country.

On the return of the party one evening, after a fatiguing day's sport through hill and dale, the worthy chief as usual threw open his castle gates, and admitted the almost worn out party. They were received with the highest courtesy, and treated with the greatest respect ; and on the pressing solicitation of Lochiel, Huntly and the other guests consented to pass the night under the chieftain's hospitable roof, for whom a splendid feast was ordered to be speedily prepared, to which a few of Lochiel's most respectable neighbours were hastily summoned. At the groaning board, on the right of Huntly, sat their brave and hospitable host and son, and on the left Lochiel's lady and her lovely daughter. The piper, as customary, played during the repast, some family airs. All, with one exception, were as joyful and happy as could be ; the ruby cup passed round, relieved with some of Ossian's songs bursting powerfully and melodiously on the ear, and at times the piobrach's stirring strains resounded through the banqueting-hall. But there was one individual present for whom the cup held out no enticement, or the rapturous songs delight, nor could the wild and martial notes of the great bagpipe arouse him from his reverie. This solitary exception was Redcastle's son, who, from the first glance he got of Lochiel's beautiful daughter, became desperately in love with her ; and although his father, who was surprised at his unusual silence, would now and then gently chide him, it had no effect in awakening him from his contemplative mood. Next morning as the guests were leaving the hospitable mansion, under the roof of which such an agreeable and happy night had been passed, each and all of them shook Lochiel and the rest of the family heartily by the hand ; and among the last to perform this mark of friendship was the laird of

Redcastle's son. He shook Lochiel and his lady with the accustomed cordiality and respect, but upon approaching Miss Cameron, the chief's daughter, to take his leave of her, there was a hesitation in his manner, his cheek was flushed, and in the expression of his eye there was an eloquence which told the throbbings of of his heart, although his tongue was mute. The young lady was also much fluttered, her colour came and went, and she hung down her eyes upon the ground until their hands separated, and the young laird was about to depart, when she ventured to raise them, and they encountered his as they were taking a last lingering loving look of the object of his affections. The declaration on either part, although not a word was spoken, was inexpressibly intelligent—the eyes spoke unutterable things, and the bond of mutual attachment was sealed. The young laird departed in melancholy silence, and quickly rejoined his party, and a few more days saw himself aud his father in safety at Redcastle.

Since the morning he had left Lochiel's, the young man was never known to be happy, it was the smile of one who was a stranger to cheerfulness—a sort of melancholy seemed to have taken possession of his mind, and settled there. This state of matters could not long remain concealed from the eye of a fond and anxious parent, who became greatly alarmed, when he discovered traces of decline in his son's countenance, and pressed him hard to know the cause. To his father's entreaties to be informed of the change in his manner, he at last yielded, and informed him of his attachment to Miss Cameron, and that without her he could not survive much longer, at the same time requesting his father to intercede for him with Lochiel. Finding that his son's affections were irretrievably fixed on Miss Cameron, Redcastle, like a wise and prudent parent, entered into the feelings of his son, and instantly despatched a trusty messenger with a letter to Lochiel, acquainting him with the distressed condition of his son, stating, at the same time, that nothing on earth would give him greater pleasure than that that chieftain would condescend to bestow his daughter on his son, and pointing out the disastrous results to himself (Redcastle) in the event of his refusing to do so. Lochiel found his daughter in much the same state as Redcastle his son, and the sooner the youthful pair were united, the better. Great was the joy of the son when Redcastle informed him of the purport of the letter, and even the worthy parent could not refrain from participating in his beloved son's happiness, at the approaching alliance with the daughter of the chief of a powerful clan.

Redcastle and his son, accompanied with a good many relatives, and a numerous body of followers, lost no time in setting out for the castle of Lochiel, where, in a few days after their arrival, the young and loving pair were united. In the evening of that eventful day, and for many after, the halls of Lochiel's castle overflowed with guests, all hearts joining in wishing happiness to the youthful couple, for which the latter seemed to entertain no fears for a bright future. During the marriage feast, the visitors were delighted with music, resounding through the extensive hall; while their followers, forgetting old animosities, betook themselves to sports and games upon the green, and were amply refreshed with home-brewed ale, etc.

After spending some weeks at Lochiel Castle the happy pair, accompanied by their friends and followers, returned to Redcastle—Lochiel sending along with his daughter his faithful and trusty valet, Donald Cameron, *an gille maol dhu*, or the bonnetless lad. Valets then, did not, as now, wear fine hats with gold and silver bands around them, neither were they dressed in any other livery than their plain clan tartan, and were not only bonnetless but shoeless. Now, although Donald Cameron held this menial situation under his chief, he was a member of one of the most respectable families in Lochaber, and nearly allied to the chief himself. It was not generally the poorest who held the situation of their chief's *gille maol dhu*, and Donald being a stately, fine looking, powerful, and faithful man, possessed no small share of Lochiel's confidence. Although Lochiel was overjoyed at his daughter's marriage with Red-castle's son, he had yet his fears for her safety, owing to an old feud that existed between the the Black Isle people and those of Lochaber, especially the Glengarry men, and the horrible tragedy at the church of Gilchrist not being yet effaced from the memory of the Black Islanders.* What still more increased his apprehensions was, that some time previous to this they were repeatedly harassed by a lawless band of cattle lifters from Lochaber—the Bains, or Macbeans, headed by their savage leader, Bengie Macbean,

* The following interesting note relative to the " Raid of Cillichriost " is from an original MS. in possession of the editor of this volume :—

" The long and sanguinary feud between the Mackenzies and the Macdonalds, and more particularly the Glengarry branch of them, is supposed to have originated in the partition of property. Be that as it may, many and deadly were the conflicts between them previous to the Raid of Cilli-chriost. The Maclellans—a tribe who acknowledged the lords of Kintail as superiors, and found protection under their banners—unfortunately intercepted and murdered the eldest son of Donald Macangus, *alias* Donald Gruimach, of Glengarrù. Donald, ere he could mature matters for ade-quate retaliation, died, and the second son (who was now chief of his clan), was, in consequence of his tender age, in-capable of heading an enterprise of sufficient importance to avenge the murder of his brother. But though the matter lay dormant for some time, and the young chief had in the buoyancy peculiar to youth, nearly forgot his sorrows, still there was one in whose rugged soul delay had but strength-ened revenge. This was Allan-dhu-Macranuil of Lundi, the chief's cousin, and, during his minority, acted as captain or leader of his clan. This man, whose personal prowess equalled his ferocity, collected the Macdonells, and several

whose son, whilst quite a youth, became so disgusted with the barbarous life his father and his adherents led, that he fled from, and never returned to them again, but afterwards became one of the brightest ministers that Scotland could boast of since the days of the great Mr Welsh. As already stated, Lochiel being aware

times swept away the Mackenzies' cattle; but these incursions were but a prelude to the more sanguinary deed in contemplation. Blood—the life-blood of a whole host of his bitterest foemen—could alone expiate the murder of his relative and chief. In singling out a favourable opportunity for his revenge, it is affirmed that he wandered for some time in the country of the Mackenzies as a mendicant, until he fixed on the scene of his horrible tragedy. Returning to his own country, he gathered a band of the most desperate of his clan, and by a forced march across the hills surrounding the church of Cillichriost, on a Sunday forenoon, when a numerous congregation had assembled to worship their common God, here, without a moment's pause—without a single pang of remorse—he ordered the infernal torches to be applied to the dry heath with which the building was thatched; and whilst a low breeze from the east fanned the work of destruction, the voice of praise from within might be heard mingling with the crackling of the flames. Too conscious at last of the awfulness of their situation, the horrified assembly rushed towards the porch. But here a double row of bristled swords were opposed to the breasts of those who thought themselves more than fortunate in having reached it. From the doorway they tumultuously flew to the small and high windows; but here, also, the same formidable barrier gleamed upon their eyes. Now indeed, arose the wild wail of despair. The shrieks of the women, the infuriated roaring of the men, and the helpless cries of the children mingled with the raging of the flames, formed a combination of horrors which appalled even the hearts of the followers of Allan-dhu Macranuil. 'Thrust them back into the flames,' said that fiend; 'he who suffers aught

of a deep-rooted prejudice existing in the minds of the Black Isle people towards the Lochaber men, made him the more anxious of sending with his daughter the *gille maol dhu*, knowing full well that this trusty adherent, sword in hand, would die in defence of his beautiful mistress. The party at length, without the least occurrence worth mentioning, arrived in safety at Redcastle, where a sumptuous banquet was prepared, to which all the neighbouring gentry and farmers were invited, and a cordial welcome the young pair received to their future home from those assembled. The surrounding hills were all in flames, every knowe showed its bonfire in honour of the occasion, and as the blaze was reflected from the Beauly and Moray Firths, Donald Cameron was convinced, that for his young mistress no danger need be apprehended from the Black Islanders, from this display of their attachment to the house of Redcastle. Donald was soon presented with a more civilised dress, with the additional appendages of bonnet and shoes. Being a remarkably

with his life to escape out of Cillichriost shall be branded as a traitor to his clan.' And they were thrust back, or hewn mercilessly down in that narrow archway until the dead opposed an insurmountable heap to the dying. Anxious to make a last desperate effort for the preservation of their suffocating young, the scorched mothers flung their infants out at the windows in the vain hope that the feelings of a father might be stirred in the bosoms of some of the savages of Lundi ; but here they were received on the broadsword, and their innocent spirits fled in the hands of monsters in

good-looking young man, he attracted the attention of the housekeeper, who was also young and pretty. Honest Donald being aware of the bonnie damsel's partiality for him, like a good and true knight, could not suffer any lady to die for love of him, and they were soon united. Having now possessed himself of an agreeable and happy companion, Donald was resolved to return to " Lochaber no more," but fix his residence in the Black Isle, and by the kindness of his amiable mistress and her lord, he was enabled to enter into possession of the farm of Mulchaich in Ferrintosh, but was not long tenant of it when he was deprived of his wife who left him, however, a legacy of seven beautiful daughters. Donald soon married again, and his second wife bore him seven sturdy sons, who grew up and married, so that the Black Isle was well supplied with the race of the *gille maol dhu.* He lived himself to a great age, and was interred in the churchyard of Ferrintosh, where also repose the ashes of many of his descendants. The descendants of the *gille maol dhu* were not only to be found in the Black Isle, but Ross-shire in general, and not a few of them are to be found in the shires of Sutherland and Moray, and even in various parts of the globe, holding prominent stations in society, while a good many respectable and

whose breasts mercy never had the smallest share. It was a wild and fearful sight, but the excess of its horrors was only witnessed by a wild and fearful race."

sturdy sons are yet to be found in Ferrintosh, their original soil.

But to return from this digression to the Mackenzies of Redcastle. The family continued to increase in wealth and power. The old castle became too old or too inconvenient, and the present castle was erected. It is situated on a small eminence within a few hundred yards of the sea, and commands one of the most extensive, varied, and picturesque views in the north. Immediatey in front is Loch Beauly, the whole of which, from the village of Beauly at the one end, to the ferry at Kessock at the other, can be seen from the castle windows. Beyond Loch Beauly, the Aird, Bunchrew, Muirtown, and Belladrum, rise in variegated splendour, with their handome seats, fruitful fields and beautiful plantations, while to the north the eye gleams along a fertile and cultivated country, until the view is bounded by the dark mountains of Strathorrin and Strathconan. The Castle itself is an extensive, commodious, and elegant structure, combining some of the conveniences of the modern mansion with the strength, the turrets, spires, loopholes, and battlements of the castles of the 16th century.

From the period when this castle was erected, the tide of prosperity which had hitherto attended the Mackenzies of Redcastle began to ebb. The superstition of the people of the country ascribed the decay of the family to the circumstance of a man having been buried alive below the foundation stone. It is unnecessary to say that there can be no grounds for a story which would reflect such diabolical disgrace on the family; but it may have arisen from the accidental death of one of the workmen while engaged in his work. The people in the neighbourhood—perhaps the most superstitious in the kingdom—required then, and require even now, but very slender materials to impose upon themselves, and upon others, a tale of horror. Be this, however, as it may, certain it is, that from that period the family declined in prosperity, until it gradually became extinct. The lairds of Redcastle, like their neighbours, took part in the civil commotions of the last century; and like most of those who were engaged in those commotions, suffered for their loyalty or disloyalty, whichever it may be called.

The last laird of Redcastle of the name of Mackenzie was Collector of Customs at Inverness, and well known to the narrator. He was a most amiable man, condescending in his manners, and arduous in the duties of his office, but from the circumstance of his eldest son Kenneth joining himself with a band of determined smugglers, the good old gentleman was viewed with a jealous eye. Kenneth was not long associated with this lawless band when he had the boldness to bring them with him to his father's castle of Redcastle, and there for safety deposit their contraband goods.

The worthy laird his father, who was not till

then aware of the illegal and evil career his son
was pursuing, although at the same time his
hopes were far from being sanguine regarding
him, as from his youth upwards he was of an
over-rambling disposition.   However, there was
now no alternative for Collector Mackenzie
but to resign his situation—a situation he
filled with honour and integrity.   He was
much felt for and sympathised with by both
high and low throughout the north, and particularly so by the inhabitants of Inverness.
Kenneth, seeing what his folly brought his
venerable parent to, he, like the prodigal son, immediately abandoned his iniquitous career.   A
short time after this he commenced the droving
trade—a more lawful occupation—but not being
successful, he gave it up for the more honourable one of fighting for his king and country,
having got a commission in the 78th, or
Ross-shire Highlanders.   So keen and eager
was he in enlistment, that he forced several
poor fellows out of their beds on his father's
estate, to accompany him to India's shores.
This work of compulsion he even had the boldness to carry on in Inverness, where he trepanned
not a few, among whom there was one of the
name of Gunn, whose mother was a reputed
witch, and whose awful imprecations were
fearfully levelled against him and his family for
tearing away her only child.   Some time after,
while with his regiment in India, he was
charged at the instance of the Government with

fraud, for which he was called home and confined for the rest of his lifetime in the Tower of London. In the midst of grief and sorrow his venerable parent calmly and meekly resigned his spirit into the hand of his eternal Father, in whose mansions the cares, toils, and disappointments of this world below are not known. The estate subsequently became much burdened, and as the second son John, who was in the army, and was much beloved and respected by his brother officers and every one who had the pleasure of his acquaintance, was not in circumstances to redeem it, it was put up for sale. A wealthy scion of the clan offered largely for it, and the only impediment in the way of getting it was his being the son of a tinker (but he was a good and honest man, although horn spoon-making, etc. was his calling), It was, however, purchased by the Grants, then by Sir William Fettes, and after his death by the present proprietor, Colonel Baillie of Tarradale, the Lord-Lieutenant of the county.

The last of the Mackenzies of Redcastle, Miss Mary or Molly, died at a very advanced old age a few years ago at Lettoch, in a house which she had occupied there for many years. She was a stately dignified old maiden lady, but somewhat eccentric in her habits, and if a story current of her in the neighbourhood be true, a little whimsical in her tastes. If the cooking of any dish did not please her, she invariably exclaimed, " Very good for servants, but don't like it for mysel'." So frequently did she give utterance to this expression, that for several years before her death the neighbours were in the habit of calling her by the title of " Very good for servants, but don't like it for mysel'." Major Mackenzie of Kincraig is the lineal descendant and representative of the Mackenzies of Redcastle.

There is, perhaps no property in Scotland which has been so much improved as the estate of Redcastle. Eighty years ago the estate was a naked barren waste, scarcely yielding any corn except on what was called the Mains. It is now one of the best cultivated properties in the kingdom, and so greatly and so rapidly did the value of the property increase in consequence of planting the hills and cultivating the plains, that although the property was purchased by the Grants only a few years before the beginning of the present century for somewhere about £20,000, it was in 1828 or 1829* sold to Sir William Fettes for the sum of about £135,000! but the present proprietor purchased it for a smaller sum. One of its most valuable farms is the ferry of Kessock, which pays a rent of about £1000 per annum, although not sixty years ago the toll was principally paid in bannocks! It is still more gratifying to record that the comfort, intelligence, and morals of the inhabitants have improved in a ratio corresponding with the value of the soil.

* For changes of proprietors see note to page 119.

Until within a late period superstition abounded in this and the neighbouring estate of Drynie. There is scarcely a bog, burn, or lonely spot with which some tale of superstitious horror is not associated ; and in addition to the ordinary witches, warlocks, ghosts, benshees, and benaives the superstitious have called to their aid the water-horse and the water-bull, which are said to frequent Loch Drynie and Linne-a-Bhuic-Bhain.

A very singular story is told of the Patersons of Kessock. It is said that one of them was fortunate and courageous enough to secure and take home a mermaid, which he kept for some time in his house. But the nymph of the ocean, being eager to regain her native element, supplicated her captor for her release, and said she would grant any three requests he would make if he would permit her to depart. He agreed to this, and one of the three which he asked was " that no Paterson should ever be drowned in the ferry of Kessock." The people of Kessock, Craigton, and Redcastle, firmly believe in this story, and their belief is strongly confirmed by the singular fact, that although many persons of the name of Paterson have for centuries been engaged on the ferry, such a circumstance as one being drowned was never known, and what is perhaps more singular is, that while the ferry was in their possession, no person was drowned in it.*

* We have heard a version of this tradition differing

Besides the above annoyance to the peaceable
inhabitants of Redcastle, they were often
troubled, especially in their sojournings under
cover of night, with other and still more wicked
demons, particularly while passing a burn about
a mile to the east of Redcastle, for scarcely one
could pass or repass it without being in danger
of their life. The last individual who was attacked at this unhallowed spot was a worthy
man of the name of Paterson, reader and catechist of the parish. Episcopacy was then the
creed of the entire district. He being at the

from the above. It was told that one of the Patersons,
taking an early stroll along the rocky shore at Craigton, had
suddenly come upon a mermaid who was disporting herself
out of her native element, and seized on her before she could
find her way back. Paterson was aware of the superstition
attached to the mermaid, that, if a scale or two were taken
off her tail she would lose the fishy part of her power. Her
captor suddenly acted on his knowledge, and immediately
before him stood a beautiful woman. He took her to his
home—married her—she bore him a family. The scales
detached from her were carefully hid away by her husband
—well knowing as he did, that if once regained by his wife,
she would resume her original state. The children were
growing up; and one day a son, who wondered what his
father's visits to a certain out-house portended, discovered
that there was something carefully put away in a place in
the wall. He one day took out the carefully wrapped-up
scales, and rushing into the house in his father's absence
showed them to his mother, who immediately seized on
them, and hurried down to the beach and disappeared in
the water. Her husband on his return home learned what
had occurred, and long mourned the mother of his children.
It is said that for years after, the family never wanted for a
daily supply of fish of all kinds—a liberal supply was always
to be found on the beach opposite their house.

time on a catechising mission in the west, and returning rather late to his own house at Easter Kessock, was attacked whilst approaching the said burn by a huge monster, and were it not for the repeated interposition of a faithful mastiff, he would never return to tell the tale. However, the poor man proceeded homewards, when there appeared as it were, a lighted torch or candle, as an emblem of the fiendish spirit being overcome, which light stuck by him until he arrived at his own house, a distance of four miles. He ordered his wife to give plenty of food to his faithful companion the dog, but next morning the poor animal was found dead, and the inference was, that although the evil spirit did not get the power over the honest catechist, it assuredly got it over his companion. Nothing daunted, the worthy man repaired next night to the burn, travelling the whole night up and down from one end to the other, carrying in his hand an open Bible, and constantly engaged in prayer. From that time henceforward, the poor traveller was never known to meet with any impediment at this ill-fated spot.

"The prayer of the righteous availeth much."

However, the march of civilisation, religious and moral, has now, we may say, entirely banished all ideas of such supernatural beings out of our land.

THE BLACK WATCH,

OR FORTY-SECOND ROYAL HIGHLANDERS, ETC.

AT the period when the Highlands were go-
verned more by might than either by
justice or honour, lawless bands of freebooters and cattle-lifters committed sad depredations on friends and foes, rich and poor. To
such excess were matters carried with a high
and daring hand, that at last their deeds of
spoliation became intolerable, threatening many
with utter ruin ; and although small detach-
ments of soldiers were stationed in garrisons in
different localities in the Highlands, they were
not of sufficient strength to cope with the hardy
and daring cattle-lifters, aided, as they generally
were in their movements and flights, by a
thorough knowledge of every nook and corner
in the whole country. To counteract their lawless and annoying deeds, and render some security to life and property, many of our Highland
chieftains and lairds found it necessary to raise
companies of strong, resolute, and able-bodied
men, acquainted with the country—each respective gentleman maintaining the company he had

raised—and whose duties were generally performed by night in scouring the country, searching for stolen cattle, or intercepting the marauders with their "*creach*," and restoring them to their owners.* The dress of the different companies was of a similar description, being dark green jacket, philabeg, hose, and brogues with large buckles, black belt over the shoulders, another round the waist, a large broadsword on the one side, and a dirk on the other —hence they were called the " Black Watch," or *Freacadain Dhu*. They sometimes carried muskets, and it may also be said they were a kind of rifle corps. Their vigilance, determination, and prowess soon struck terror and alarm into the hearts of the evil-doers, and their very name carried fear with it, so that ere long depredations were scarcely heard of, and at last existed only in the mere name. An effectual check being thus given to the freebooters, it was considered unnecessary to continue the Black Watch any longer ; but, nevertheless, as they were such useful, brave, and excellent bands of men, it was thought a hardship to dis-

* The Government of the day established these independent companies in 1729. They were paid and maintained by the authorities, and not by the Highland chiefs. The notorious Simon Lord Lovat was in command of one company, and it has been said that the deprivation of this military honour in 1744 led him to plunge deeper into the intrigues of the Jacobite party. Colonel Grant of Ballindalloch and George Munro of Culcairn were other northern lairds who had commands given to them in this local force.

band them, particularly as their country at the time required the services of all able to carry arms in its defence—and these men, if formed into a regiment, would make a very superior one. To suggest such to these brave men would be inconsistent with the motives which embodied them, and not altogether safe. But the chiefs and lairds, being bent on forming them into a regiment, had recourse to artifice and flattery. Accordingly, in April 1744, the different companies were assembled in Inverness; but the object for which they were called together was of course kept a profound secret. At Inverness, all the companies were embodied into one, and non-commissioned officers of the "regulars" were procured to drill them every day, and train them in the proper army exercises. They remained a considerable time in Inverness, were put "through their facings" daily, and learning the different military manœuvres, at last, naturally supposing that their services being now no longer required, they would be allowed to return to their homes and families; but no—they were otherwise destined. The place where they used to exercise is a little to the south of the Ness Islands, still known as Campfield.

Artifice and flattery, as stated, were necessary to induce the Black Watch to leave the vicinity of their homes. They were told by their chiefs and officers, that his Majesty, hearing of their fine appearance, and the great services they had done the country, was anxious to make a personal inspection of such a distinguished body of men previous to their being disbanded. The duped Black Watch, elated with such a message from royalty, unanimously consented to embark for London, on the understanding that after the review they would be sent home to their families.* However, a melancholy occurrence happened which threw a sad gloom over the whole corps, and was construed by many as a bad omen. One of Lord Lovat's company had been for some time paying his addresses to a young female in the town, who became *enciente.* Pretending to be going to the Aird to bid adieu to his parents, he requested the confiding girl to accompany him on his paternal message, that he might introduce her as his intended partner for life, and on their return to town he would have their union solemnized. Cheered by the prospect of an immediate union, and relying on his assurances, the unfortunate girl consented to accompany him. On the road thither, they called at Peggy Bain

---

* When the regiment assembled at Perth in March 1743, they learned with surprise of the intention to send them to England, and thereafter abroad to reinforce the army in Flanders. After protestations and the warnings of Lord President Forbes, the Government persisted, and they were marched to London. These proceedings were attended by disaster, and resulted in the desertion of a large body of the men, who attempted a retreat to Scotland. We need not follow this episode ;—but finally the soldiers were induced to return to their duty. Three of the ringleaders in this affair were tried and found guilty, and were shot.

the innkeeper's, at Clachnaharry, where they had a glass of gin or hollands. Here they remained for a considerable time, he being evidently anxious to prolong their stay as much as he could, and, intending not to go much farther with his unsuspecting victim, was wishful that the shades of night would close and shroud the diabolical deed he contemplated. They started at last for the Aird, but, alas! horrid to relate, the Aird she was destined never to reach, for they only reached Bunchrew, and there, close to the roadside, beneath the foliage of an alder tree, the poor unfortunate girl was barbarously murdered by her inhuman seducer. In about an hour after the tragical deed was done, he was in Peggy Bain's again, and had a dram. Seeing him besmeared with blood, Peggy suspected what had occurred, and asked what had become of his companion, and how far he had accompanied her; but he would return no answer, and hastily left for town. Next day the mangled corpse of the deluded female was found in the spot where she had been murdered. The Black Watch man, understanding that he was generally suspected, precipitately fled to the hills and fastnesses of the Aird, supposing that among his clan he would be secure, and which he certainly was for some time, for they aided him greatly, and thereby eluded those sent in pursuit. President Forbes, who was at the time in Edinburgh, hearing of the murder, and of its being committed near his favourite residence, wrote

Lord Lovat, stating, that he hoped none of his clan would shelter or screen an individual guilty of such an atrocious crime, besides, that he had written to Inverness, in order that a party of the 15th Foot, then stationed in the Castle, would go to the Aird and capture the murderer, if possible. This had the desired effect for the murderer was soon taken, tried, and sentenced to death. He confessed the crime, and acknowledged the justice of his sentence., The alder tree never again shot forth leaves, but for years stood a withered stump, as if bearing testimony to the atrocity of the crime perpetrated under it. The narrator well remembers seeing this tree.

Whilst the above distressing events were being enacted, the Black Watch left in great glee for the Metropolis. They were reviewed by his Majesty * and principal officers, and high were the encomiums passed on them. After satisfying the curiosity of the cockneys, they were marched to Chatham, where they were to embark for the Continent. At Chatham they understood the turn matters had taken, and that they were not to be allowed to return to their peaceful homes as promised, but to fight with Britain's foes. A good many here deserted, but most were captured, a few only making good their escape. Britain was then waging war with France, and the first appearance of the Black

---

* This is not a fact. The King left for Hanover the same day that the Highlanders reached the outskirts of London.

Watch on the Continent was at the memorable battle of Fontenoy. Here they were placed where the battle raged the hottest; but seeing the slight damage done to the enemy's ranks by their muskets, they seemed to waver, which being noticed by their companions, thought they meant to desert, and were therefore preparing to fire upon them, but they were sadly mistaken; desertion they knew not or dreamed of, for throwing away their cumbersome muskets, and drawing their claymores, the Black Watch,

"True to the last of their blood and their breath,
And, like reapers, descend to the harvest of death,"

dashed instantly amongst the enemy, whose line, by the impetuosity of the charge, they soon broke, and made fearful carnage. At this time a party of dragoons rode up, and followed the advantage gained by the Black Watch, to whose bravery and undaunted courage the victory was mainly ascribed. Of them the French commander remarked, "Oh! how these royal bonnets slaughter our men," which being reported by the Duke of Cumberland, commander of the British forces, to his Majesty, the latter said, "Then let them be henceforward royal." This memorable battle was fought on 30th April 1745. Subsequently the cause of the Pretender was exciting some alarm, and it was thought advisable to recall the Duke of Cumberland with a considerable part of his forces; but although the

Black Watch, now the 42nd Royal Highlanders, had distinguished themselves, they were not allowed to return, Government fearing that once more on their native hills, they would not fight for the House of Hanover against their chiefs and relations, who fought in Prince Charlie's cause. This was probably a judicious step, and not even affording them an opportunity of testing their loyalty. It is but justice to say that the 42nd, throughout all the wars up to 1815, distinguished itself as a brave, valiant, and renowned corps, which their innumerable laurels amply testify.

DONALD GRUIMACH.

THE BLACK ISLE CATTLE-LIFTER.

F OR the last two centuries there has not, perhaps, been a more notorious cattle-lifter
than Donald Gruimach. From his very
grim and ferocious appearance, he was better
known by the *soubriquet* of " Gruimach." Indeed, Donald was the terror of the whole
country, especially the Black Isle, to which his
depredations were chiefly confined, and whose
lairds he most unsparingly plundered of their
best cattle and sheep. He resided near Tarradale, and never walked abroad without his *bitac*
(dirk) and *skian dhu*. His courage was as
reckless as his presence of mind was astonish-
ing, and being thoroughly acquainted with the
locale of the scene of his operations (for there
was not a corner or crevice in the country with
which he was not familiar), it rendered it no
easy task to bring home any charge to him.
And although many were quite conscious that

he, and he alone, was the person who stole their cattle and sheep—still they were afraid to lay such an action to the credit of this renowned freebooter. However, M'Homais, the laird of Applecross, whose sheep now and then were stolen from off his estate of Highfield (which was then, and for many years after, the property of the Applecross family),* determined to make a strict and thorough investigation respecting his stolen property, and Donald's fame reaching his ears, it naturally occurred to him that there was none so likely to harass him as Donald Gruimach ; consequently he despatched twelve strong able-bodied men to Donald's bothy on the evening of the day on which one of his best wedders disappeared. Donald, however, happened to be about the door, and as the guilty mind is always timorous and apprehensive of coming evil, he gave a cautious look around his residence, then with the keen and penetrating glance of the eagle scanned the face of the country, where he espied at a distance the men rapidly approaching him. He saw portending danger in their movements, and there being no time to lose in conjecture as to the purport of their mission, he instantly entered his hut, seized the sheep and bound it with thongs,—then laid it in a large cradle, and covering it over with a piece of blanket, he seated

---

* The estate of Highfield was sold by the Mackenzies in 1781.

himself beside it, and appeared tenderly engaged in rocking the supposed child, humming at the same time, "*Baloo, baloo, mo lenaibh ! !*" while the men made their entrance at the door. One of them accosted Donald by asking, "Where is the wedder you have taken to-day from High-field?" He answered them quite seriously, and not the least disconcerted, "May I eat him that's in the cradle, if I took it." They did not question Donald further, or examine the contents of the cradle, by which he swore so fervently, but returned much mortified, without taking either sheep or Donald ; and it may easily be supposed that he was but too happy when he saw them make their exit, and get so easily out of this uncomfortable dilemma. But this narrow escape from detection had no effect on Donald, neither did it prevent his levying contributions on those in the neighbourhood of his abode, for sometime thereafter he had the hardihood to take one of Kilcoy's best oxen from the Mains ; but whether it was owing to his being always so well armed, or that the proof against him was considered inadequate to ensure a conviction, there was no effort at the time made to take him into custody,—he was, therefore, for some time suffered to roam undisturbed over the country, committing several other depredations.

Kilcoy, however, did not forget the loss of his good ox, but it availed not ; he could not fall on any scheme to entrap the wary thief.

After running over in his mind several strata-
gems, which were no sooner concocted than dis-
pelled, he at last thought on the following.
Being told that Donald was in the vicinity of
the Castle, he went out, in order, if possible, to
meet or see him, and was not long in discovering the object of his search. Donald, seeing
Kilcoy approach him unaccompanied, stood,
for indeed he was so powerful that he would
not show his back to the four strongest men in
the country. Kilcoy told him he had an important letter to send to the Sheriff at Fortrose,
which required urgent attention, and that if he
would convey it, he would get a shilling for his
trouble, which in those times was considered no
bad remuneration for the distance he had to
travel. Donald hesitated, but at last consented
to go. Kilcoy then immediately went and
wrote the necessary letter to the Sheriff, the
purport of which was that the bearer was a
most notorious stealer of cattle and sheep, and
that it would be doing the greatest service to
the country at large, if he (the Sheriff) on re-
ceipt would safely secure Donald in jail, as
shortly charges would be brought against him
which would be proved to his satisfaction; as
himself and many of his neighbours around
him, suffered severely from the redoubtable
cattle-lifter.

Donald could neither read nor write; however, he did not proceed far on his way, wrapt
in meditation, his own circumstances haunting

his mind, and probably contemplating the reckless career of his past life, when he began to
examine and look very minutely into the letter,
when, lo ! he imagined that in it he discovered
the horns of Kilcoy's brown ox.   It then occurred to him that it was for the purpose of
having himself apprehended and handed over to
the Sheriff, that he was despatched with the
letter, which was meant to have effected this
object.   He immediately retraced his steps,
and the first person he met was the laird himself, who, no doubt, was previously overjoyed
at the thought of ridding himself of such a formidable neighbour as Donald Gruimach.   But
in this the laird of Kilcoy was sadly disappointed, who, addressing Donald, asked him,
" How was it that he returned so soon ? "
Donald's mind was not at rest, and he answered
the laird, " Back ! it is no wonder than I am
back; did I not see the very horns of the
brown ox in that letter as distinct as possibly
could be ? "   Then, throwing the ominous
letter at Kilcoy's feet, fled with the swiftness of
the roe to his hiding-place, in order to elude
the search of any who might be sent in pursuit
of him.

Crime may be carried on unchallenged for a
time, but a day of reckoning will come, when
justice will prevail, and so it happened with
Donald.   He was seized for stealing a stot from
a widow who lived on the estate of Tulloch—
Bayne being then the proprietor, who warmly

interested himself in the poor woman's loss. Donald was lodged in Dingwall jail, and while he lay there, the widow visited him daily, furnishing him with the best meat she could procure, in order if possible, by her kindness, to extract some information from him, by which she could recover her favourite stot. He always promised to tell her where the stot was, and thereby kept her in continual suspense. In due time he was tried and sentenced to be executed. On the day of his execution, and while he stood on the platform, the poor woman cried out to him, " Will you no tell me now where is my stot ? " But he answered, " I have more to think of at present than you or your stot." While he thus stood he was anxiously and impatiently looking towards the west, as he expected a strong party of the clan Fraser to make their appearance and effect a rescue. They actually left their homes for that purpose, and came the length of Ord, but having been met there by a number of the Mackenzies as a deputation from Brahan Castle, the latter reasoned with them on the necessity and justice of freeing the country of such a notorious individual as Donald Gruimach, and prevailed on the Frasers to return, without proceeding farther to rescue him from the scaffold, a doom which he so justly merited. Donald was never known to commit any encroachment on the Lovat estates, and it was supposed that it was on this account the

Frasers favoured him so much. One of his most impregnable hiding-places was on the estate of Lovat in Glenstrathfarar, and it was further conjectured that he was a scion of that clan.

HIGHLAND ROBBERS AND CATTLE-LIFTERS.

THE following is an account of the wild and daring exploits of three of the most hardy cattle-lifters that ever traversed our Highland hills, viz., Alexander Macdonald, *alias* Coire-na-Caorach; Donald Kennedy or Mac-ourlic, *alias* An Gaduiche Dubh; and Samuel Cameron, *alias* Mac Domhuil Dubh :—

Macdonald, or Coire-na-Caorach, lived in a secluded bothy on the confines of the Glengarry estate, a little to the west of Fort-Augustus, whose daring exploits in robbery and cattle-lifting ultimately became the terror and scourge of the surrounding country, whose *creach*, or spoil, he often, in defiance of the law, drove to the south. However, this state of things was not to be much longer carried on by him, as the neighbouring lairds supposed, with their vassals combined, they might lay hold of him; and none was more eager for his apprehension than Glengarry, who cordially joined the other lairds in getting him outlawed; but Coire-na-Caorach being apprised of their design, it only had the effect of making him more vigilant than before. Coire now perceiving that he was outlawed and a price set upon his head, determined on not venturing any more to sojourn over night at his own residence, but ever afterwards took up his nightly abode in his cave on the margin of Loch Ness, a most rugged and craggy spot, a few miles west of the celebrated Falls of Foyers. This cave actually stretches out upwards of twenty yards below the bed of the lake, and over the entrance was a large flagstone.   There Coire-na-Caorach was perfectly secure from all his pursuers, where he lived on the best, viz., roast beef and mutton, etc., but he contrived to see his wife now and then in her bothy without being observed ; at last, in consequence of old age creeping upon him, he became unable any longer to go in search of prey, and confined himself to his dungeon.   At length he became so very ill that she expressed her wish that he should breathe his last under their own roof. But how was this to be done ?   About midnight, however, this devoted woman buckled up the feeble frame of her husband in a good blanket and carried him to the mouth of the cave, and afterwards trudged through rugged rocks and barren moors with her aged partner in life, and arrived at the house in safety—unseen and unknown—before daylight.   Coire began to sink rapidly, and in the course of a few days thereafter, breathed his last, when his remains were gathered to the dust of his kindred unmolested.

Donald Kennedy, or Macourlic, *alias* an Gaduiche Dubh, was also a notorious thief and cattle-lifter. He lived in the Braes of Lochaber, and sometimes sojourned in the company of Coire-na-Caorach, and divided the spoil. He was also outlawed, and a price set upon his head. Having no proper place of concealment in the neighbourhood, he forsook home and family, and went to Perthshire. Here he engaged as a farm servant, and a rather curious circumstance led to his discovery. A fine horse, the property of his master, having been amissing, he was ordered to search for the animal, which he gladly consented to do, and on his finding the horse, rode at Gilpin speed to a remote part of the country with it and sold it. After being two days away he returned to his master, telling him that there was not a hill or dale that he could think of but he searched for the horse. His master replied, angrily, and said, " You ought to try, sir, places you did not think of." An Gaduiche Dubh set out again on his pretended pursuit, but in the course of a few minutes thereafter, the worthy farmer and his wife, who were sitting round a blazing pile of peats, were suddenly startled by a rumbling noise on the top of the house. In a minute or two afterwards large pieces of turf began to pour down upon them, which caused them

quickly to repair outside, lest the whole fabric
might fall in, when, to their astonishment, who
did they see on the housetop (eagerly throwing
the turf in all directions around him), but he
whom they sent in further search of their horse.
The honest farmer bawled out to his servant,
"What in the world prompted you to do such
mischief?" The Gaduiche replied, "Did you
not tell me to go and search for the horse where
I did not think of, and I am just doing so."
Before morning the farmer formed another
opinion of his supposed half-witted servant, for,
said he to his wife, "As sure as you are alive,
woman, Donald is no other than the Gaduiche
Dubh (the fame of the Gaduiche being over the
length and breadth of the Highlands), so that
the sooner we get quit of him in peace and
quietness the better." The honest wife at once
coincided with her husband. Next morning
Donald was paid his wages, no doubt as well
pleased to go as his master and mistress were
to get quit of him.

At one time Lochiel being on a visit to Glengarry, where the two chiefs spent a happy night
together, among other conversation between
them a wager was laid which of the two, viz.,
an Gaduiche Dubh or Coire-na-Caorach, was
the greatest thief. Glengarry wagered on
Coire's head, and Lochiel on that of the Gaduiche. Next day the desperadoes made their
appearance before their respective chiefs at the
Castle of Glengarry. Having been told the
nature of their mission they set down the strath

to Fort-Augustus; from thence to Invermoris-
ton, but having espied nothing worthy of capturing, they traversed part of Glenmoriston
with as little success. Being determined not to
return without some evidence of their expert-
ness, they bent their course to Glen-Urquhart.
After ascending the hill of Monadh-na-Leum-
naich, Donald, the Gaduiche Dubh, became
overcome with fatigue, and said it was of no
use to enter the country of the Frasers and Mackenzies, as they would be in danger of being
taken, they then sat down on the top of that
stupendous hill, and immediately Donald fell
into a profound sleep. However, Coire-na-
Caorach did not sleep, as he was fully determined not to return without some token of his
dexterity, and having quickly unfolded his companion's plaid, cut a piece out of one of the
folds, and made a pair of hose, which he put on
his brawny legs ere he awakened the Gaduiche
Dubh. He now roused him up, saying it was
of no use to go further, but to return to Glengarry. The Gaduiche reluctantly assented, and
on their arrival at the Castle the chiefs anxiously
enquired what had they done on their journey.
The Gaduiche spoke first, and said he regretted
to say nothing at all. Coire-na-Caorach
answered, looking to Donald, " But I have
though; look at my hose, and look at your
breacan," or plaid. The Gaduiche unfolded it
and at once saw that the piece had been taken
out of it, and became fully convinced that it

was the identical piece which had been so quickly converted into Highland leggings. As a matter of course, Glengarry won the wager. The Gaduiche, like his contemporary, Coire-na-Caorach, lived to a great age, and died a natural death.

Samuel Cameron, *alias* Mac Dhomhuil Dubh, was also one of those worthies who considered might to be right, and that his ability and daring in cattle-lifting afforded him a title to pursue that vocation with impunity. At the era of the outlaw, the power of life and death was confided to the Sheriffs, and he who was the principal Sheriff in the north at this time, was a Mr Mackenzie, of the family of Kilcoy, residing at Kilmuir Wester, better known on account of his severity by the title of Shirra Dubh. This official had long desired to have Mac Dhomhuil Dubh iu his clutches, and he at length succeeded. Conviction and sentence of death followed as a necessary consequence of his having fallen into the hands of the Sheriff; but just previous to the hour of execution, Mac Dhomhuil Dubh applied his herculean powers with such success as to break out of the Inverness jail; and rendered still more desperate by this circumstance, became a greater terror than ever to the surrounding country, which he in a manner placed under tribute. The officers of justice, although they knew whereabouts his ordinary retreat was situated, at the same time knew that their lives would be in jeopardy by even approaching the supposed spot, as he could with his pistols and gun defend himself successfully against a host of invaders. A cave in the Red Craig, near Abriachan, on the mountain side above Loch-Ness, was his place of rendezvous.

From this elevated spot the outlaw could command an extensive view of the Loch, and for miles all around, particularly to the south and east of Inverness, while no one could pass along the narrow pathway at the foot of the mountain without coming under the inspection of the tenant. It happened on one occasion that Shirra Dubh was led by the chase along the side of Loch-Ness, immediately below the domicile of the outlaw, who, perched eagle-like, aloft betwixt earth and sky, and with a glance well-nigh as keen, watched the approach of a horseman in whom he quickly recognised the person of the relentless Shirra Dubh. With the delight of the vulture hovering over its devoted prey, and with the agility of the tiger advancing to spring from his lair, the person of the outlawed Highlander, with a visage so overgrown with hair as to resemble the shaggy goats that alone shared with him the empire of the mountains, might have been seen rapidly descending the face of the cliff, or screening himself behind the stunted pine and birch trees which skirted the base, until Shirra Dubh came fairly abreast of the place where he was ensconced. Then springing forward, the outlaw, with one hand, grasped with an iron clutch the neck of the Sheriff, while with the other he presented a pistol at his breast, exclaiming, "Shirra

Dubh, I have you now in my power. I am hunted like a beast from the earth; if I attempt to meet my family, I do it as the peril of being shot by any one that may please. I cannot be worse off, and now, unless you will solemnly swear to reverse my sentence, and declare me a free man at the Cross of Inverness, on Friday first, I will instantly shoot you." The Sheriff perceived that he was entirely at the mercy of the outlaw, in whose haggard countenance and eye he plainly read that desperation which would assuredly lead him to fulfil his threatening. He therefore religiously proposed compliance, but this would not satisfy Mac Domhuil Dubh, until he gave a most solemn oath, whereupon he was permitted to depart, and the outlaw retreated to his cave. Shirra Dubh, true to his oath, assembled on the following Friday (being a market-day), the officials of the town and neighbourhood, and publicly, at the Cross, proclaimed the reversal of the sentence, and Samuel Cameron, *alias* Mac Dhomhuil Dubh, a free man. This act of mercy was not misplaced, as Samuel, who had been a pest to the wealthy proprietors, and (like Rob Roy), to them only, ever after abandoned his predatory habits, and lived highly respected for the remainder of his life at the Muir of Bunchrew, where he reared up a large family. The narrator was personally acquainted with his grandson, a most decent and exemplary man.

A D D E N D A.

INVERNESS IN THE OLDEN TIME.

MUNICIPAL AFFAIRS.

PREVIOUS to the year 1775 it was customary for the whole of the Town Council to assemble on Sundays at half-past ten o'clock AM. at the Provost's house, and thence go in procession to church. After divine service was over, they returned in the same order to the Provost's residence, where they were duly solaced with a glass or two of Hollands and some bread and cheese. The town-officers, who sat on a form in the lobby, were not forgotten ; for whilst their superiors were regaling themselves up-stairs, the humble functionaries were each served with a good oat bannock and a coggie of strong beer. When the Council after this manner had made a hearty lunch, they returned in similar state to the afternoon service, after which they returned to their respective homes. This piece of civic ostentation was discontinued, and the magisterial authorities proceeded to the church from the Town Hall, as at present, in consequence of a dispute as to precedance and dignity. The dispute happened in this way. A little tailor residing at Drakies, named Hugh Chisholm, had the good fortune (as it was said) to find a wallet well filled with gold in a whin-bush near the bothy in which he resided, which was supposed to have been concealed there by an officer in the Highland army in his flight from the battlefield of Culloden.

Hugh, however, did not give up his business, but continued steadily for several years at his lawful calling at Drakies, during which many a good calf did he measure, being specially famed for making hose. He at length came to reside in Inverness, where he engaged in the profession of a merchant. He was successful in business, and attracted the attention of Provost Chisholm, who was partial to him on account of of his being a clansman ; and the result was that honest Hugh was invited to become one of the civic rulers of the Highland capital—an honour which he at once and very proudly accepted. This took place in September 1775. The seat in the High Church at present appropriated to the use of the magistrates, at that time was divided into two pews. The front one being considered the most honourable, was of course occupied by the Provost and magistrates, and the other appropriated to the merchant and trade councillors. The merchant councillors took precedence of those denominated trade councillors, and entered the pew according to their order, the tradesmen following.

The first day little Hugh joined the magisterial procession, he substituted the cocked hat for the blue broad bonnet, the single-breasted broad-skirted coat for the home-made *kelt* one, and thus conceitedly trudged along with his brother councillors. On arriving at the church, Hugh's right of precedence was disputed by Convener Grant the coppersmith—a stately, fine-looking man—who, carrying in his hand his official staff, looked upon his newly installed brother with both jealousy and contempt.

Hugh, however, determined to maintain his rights, when a regular scuffle ensued, and notwithstanding the interference of the worthy Provost, and Jock Hay and Rory Mackinnon, the burgh officers, their angry looks and threatening gestures did not subside until some minutes after the minister had entered the pulpit. This unseemly *melee* in the house of prayer caused a painful sensation in the congregation. Next day a meeting of Council was summoned, and the Convener was sharply rebuked by the Provost for persisting in what was not his right, and thus occasioning confusion in such a place and on such a day. Afterwards, on the motion of the Provost, it was resolved that the two pews should be converted into one solely for the accommodation of the Provost and magistrates, and ever since it has remained in *statu quo.** It was also resolved that the procession to church should henceforward take place from the Town Hall.

FRACAS AT CNOCAN·NA-GOUR.

Cnocan-na-Gour, or "Goat's Knowe," is a rising ground on the Tomnahurich Road about half-a-mile west of Inverness, where, about a century and a-half since, markets were held for the sale of goats. Subsequently a weekly market came to be held on this stance every Thursday afternoon for the sale of butcher meat, poultry, eggs, butter, and cheese. The sellers of these useful commodities were chiefly the Urquhart and Glenmorriston tenantry, who, by selling their goods here, evaded the payment of the bridge toll and the other customs in the town. The glens' people were from time to time well supported and patronised by the inhabitants, who resorted thither to buy, being supplied cheaper than at the regular Friday market in town, so that those who attended the latter had often to return home without selling scarcely anything, which was deemed by them

-----

* A change has again taken place in the arrangement of the magisterial pew. It has this year (1894) been formed into two seats as in 1775. The magistrates, however, now only make one visit annually to the High Church, on the first Sabbath after the election in November.

a hardship, they having to pay the regular dues.

The magistrates at length saw the injustice of the regular market being thus forestalled by the illegal one at Cnocan-na-Gour, which, if allowed to be held, would tend much to diminish the revenue of the town. A meeting of Council was called which unanimously agreed that vigorous and prompt measures should immediately be adopted so as to discontinue the Thursday market at Cnocan-na-Gour. However, they thought it more advisable, before having recourse to harsh measures that two or three of their number should on the following Thursday go thither and apprise the mountaineers in calm language of the determination of the Council respecting their assembling there. To this warning the glens' people paid a deaf ear.

The deputation returned and reported to their official brethren the equal determination of the mountaineers to resist to the utmost of their power any infringment that might be attempted on what they conceived to be their just rights. On this another meeting of Council was called, when it was resolved that the whole body, with their officers and a *posse* of constables, should proceed on the afternoon of the following Thursday to the market, and compel those assembled —sellers and buyers—never to meet again there for the same purpose. As the market people were gathering the next Thursday they were apprised of the determination of the magistrates and Council, and who were to be on the ground shortly. Notwithstanding they were nowise alarmed. At length the official dignitaries and their followers appeared in the distance, headed by the town officers with Lochaber axes on their shoulders.

The glens' people now thought it was time to put themselves in battle-array so as to meet their civic opponents. Both parties met, and in an instant a savage onslaught was the result —fist to fist and cudgel to cudgel. The burgh officers made themselves prominent with their halberds or Lochaber axes, and there was nothing now but helter-skelter—bonnets and cocked hats flying in all directions.

For some time it was uncertain which of the parties would be triumphant. At length the magistrates and their party took to their heels, some of them having received fearful scars and bruises. They were hotly pursued, and it was only those who were so fortunate as to be long-limbed that escaped scathe-less.

The most formidable and effectual weapons used by the sons of the mountain were legs of mutton, which they dexterously wielded and brandished in skelping right and left to the horror and consternation of the Inverness rulers and their assistants.

On their arrival in town the Council as-sembled and wrote immediately to the lairds of Grant and Glenmorriston, giving an account of the whole matter, who, after receiving the letter, convened their respective tenants and cottars, charging them never more to meet in the same place for the sale of their goods— whoever doing so being threatened with removal from their estates. This had the desired effect ; and so ended the Thursday's market at Cnocan-na-Gour, to the great mortification of the glens' people as well as disappointment of the townsfolk.

PROVOST MACLEAN IN A FIGHT.

Another somewhat serious affair, and akin to the preceding, took place on the High Street opposite the Cross. This occurrence happened about the year 1725. On market days it was invariably the practice of the town's boys to annoy country lads by throwing handfuls of shot, or otherwise tempting them, so as to induce them to retaliate—the town boys generally having a strong force at hand to assist them if any of their number was struck. On the occasion referred to a sturdy Highlander of the name of Maclean, from the braes of Glen-Urquhart, not relishing altogether the pranks of his beardless friends, succeeded in bringing some of them within arms length, and quickly putting four of them *hors-de combat.* Their cries soon attracted a number of their compa-

nions to their aid, and the mountaineer had soon
to deal with heavier metal, as a considerable
number of persons of more powerful strength
than those he had already encountered entered
on the fray. For a few minutes he withstood
their charge, defending himself most gallantly,
but he was ultimately overpowered. For him
there was no quarter, and he would not surren-
der. In the height of his despair, he called
out so as to be heard above the deafening noise
of the crowd—' Oh! sirs, is there not a son of
Clan Gillean here to-day ?" His appeal was
not in vain. Provost Maclean was at the moment standing in his shop-door, waiting for the
arrival of a party of constables for whom he
had sent to quell the fight, and on hearing the
distressed cry of his clansman, his Highland
blood got the ascendancy, and forgetting his
dignity as chief magistrate, he rushed bare-
headed into the crowd, clearing his way as he
advanced, and knocking down his fellow-citizens
right and left, until he made his way to the
side of his oppressed namesake.

The crowd did not perceive, until he was
planted in the midst of them, that it was the
Provost who had thus unmercifully belaboured
them ; and then his face operated like magic.
Some stood amazed, while others, quickly rea-
lising the situation, took to their heels, while
not a few bore marks of after-recognition. The
Provost took his brave and thankful namesake

by the hand, saying, " I heard your distressing cry, and at once came to your assistance, and would not count him that would not do so as a true son of Clan Gillean." He then led him to his house and entertained him hospitably, and on leaving presented him with an excellent bonnet as a further token of his esteem for the manner in which he upheld the honour of the clan,

Provost Maclean was an amiable and kind-hearted man, and in his day the principal merchant in Inverness. His shop was opposite the Exchange, in the town residence of the once powerful Cuthberts of Castlehill, otherwise known as " Tigh mor Mic Sheorsa." The late Colonel Inglis of Kingsmills was a lineal descendant in the female line of Provost Maclean.

THE BLOODY MARYMAS CHEESE MARKET.

The Marymas market for the sale of cheese in the olden time was held on the southmost end of the Castle Hill, and the last which was held there was the scene of a most sanguinary affray, arising out of a circumstance of a trifling and ludicrous nature. On a beautiful August evening in the year 1666, a stout masculine-looking dairymaid from Strathnairn, not well-satisfied with her sales, was hastily packing up her unsold kebbocks, and the discontented

manner in which she set about this was remarked ; but as ill-luck would have it, or to
torment her the more, one of the kebbocks unfortunately slipping from her hand rolled down
the green slope ; nor was its course arrested
until the waters of the Ness closed over it.

The descent of the kebbock was noticed by
two or three young boys of the town who lost
no time in snatching it from its watery bed ;
but the dairymaid, seeing it was recovered, and
and supposing the boys would, for their trouble,
appropriate it as their own, despatched a like
number of lads of her own acquaintance from
the country to take it from them. The town
boys refusing to give up the cheese, words
speediy degenerated into blows. The country
lads, having the worst of the day, a number of
grown-up people came to their aid, but this movement was followed by additional supplies pouring
in on the side of the town's people—so that in
a few minutes hundreds were engaged in the
broil, which now bore the appearance of a pitched
battle. The Provost hearing of what was going
on, hastened to the ground accompanied by the
Sheriff and a party of soldiers from the Castle ;
but their utmost exertions to put a stop to the
fight were of no avail. Their presence only in-
censed the combatants the more. Fresh supplies poured in every moment, and all kinds of
weapons that could be procured were put in use.
Town officers, with their Lochaber axes, were
opposed by the cudgels of the mountaineers.

The fight having now raged for more than three hours without either side wavering, and no more auxiliaries arriving, the combatants simultaneously desisted. Then came reflection. The river Ness was dyed with blood, and all around were heard the groans and piercing cries of the wounded, the friends and acquaintances of the combatants. Both sides were horror-struck at the work they had been engaged in, and neither could claim the victory. This battle was denominated the "kebbock battle," or *batail-a-mulachac*—a name which will not be forgotten in the annals of the Highland capital. Connected with this senseless carnage, the dairymaid, according to tradition afterwards told, that whilst the milk was yearning in the "muckle pot" for the unlucky kebbock, it actually appeared like blood; and further, that her hands and arms had been all covered over with the same. After the above conflict a cheese market was never more held in the same place, but formed part and parcel of the regular Marymas fair in the town.

SMUGGLING.

At the period we write of the protection of the revenue in the Highland capital was entrusted to two functionaries, an excise officer and a tide-waiter. These two worthies held and exercised considerable sway over the roving

desperadoes of the Highlands, but they nevertheless came into frequent collision with them
and had consequently many narrow and hair-,
breadth escapes. The fairy hill of Tomnahurich had been a favourite resort of the smugglers, although locality and other circumstances
must have rendered it extremely inconvenient
for their desperate purposes, and it is probable
they availed themselves of the superstitious
dread which was then attached to this haunted
hill, a feeling no doubt increased by their own
nocturnal orgies. No matter why, it is certain
that this was the selected spot where many an
" anker " of sparkling Hollands had been carefully deposited.

The smugglers generally employed an Ama-
zon denominated Muckle Madge, to carry
their illegal gear from Tomnahurich to the
town, and in this capacity she on one occasion unfortunately met the gauger, who, of
course, demanded the prize. Madge, however,
without revolving the propriety of the matter,
resolved to hazard an engagement, and a desperate conflict ensued, but she was no match
for the officer with his cutlass, and the result
was that victory and a cask of gin became his
pro tempore. The exciseman, however, having
plenty of other work before him was necessi-
tated to conceal his prize in a court opposite
where the Northern Meeting Rooms now
stand, but in doing so he had been perceived by
a young lad and lass who had chosen a corner

of the court to talk over certain business interesting only to themselves, and who, discovering the gauger's secret, carried off the "anker"
in triumph, and restored it to its original
owner.

Some time afterwards Archie Chisholm, another officer of the excise, was assailed at the
Little Green by a mob of young women, who
seized the officer, and having bound him in a
large washing-tub, set him adrift down the
river. Fortunately, however, his incongruous
barque took the ground whilst getting over a
shoal, and he was rescued from his perilous situation by a benevolent individual who happened to hear his cries of distress.

Another character named Rory Macquain, a
very strong and powerful man, was pretty often
employed in those times by certain authorities
to carry supplies of gin, etc., from their hiding-
place, the whin bushes of the fairy hill, into the
town. On one occasion he had the boldness to
carry a large "anker" of Hollands in broad
daylight, meeting with no interruption till he
came to the bridge, on the parapet of which he
rested his heavy burden. Here he espied little
Mr Hossack the tide-waiter coming in great
haste in his direction. Rory was a good deal
down in the mouth, but determined to make a
bold stroke for the gin, and as his enemy the
tide-waiter came quite close, Rory accosted
him with—"I wish, Mr Hossack, you would

relieve me of this weighty 'anker' of gin, as I am perfectly tired with carrying it," to which honest Mr Hossack answered—"Don't you be mocking me, Rory, for weel ken I you have no such thing in that 'anker.'" Rory was allowed to pass the rest of his way without molestation, and delivered his valuable burden to its proper owner. What is most singular, Mr Hossack was well aware of Rory's notoriety as a smuggler, but never thought he would have had the hardhood to indulge in such a practice at midday. But in those days almost all respectable householders brewed their own ale, which no doubt led Mr Hossack to think that it was an "anker" of such beverage Rory Macquain was carrying.

SHERIFFS CAMPBELL AND FRASER OF INVERNESS-SHIRE.

Perhaps a more upright and merciful judge than Sheriff Campbell never sat upon the bench, or one who took a greater interest in the cases of the humbler classes. At the commencement of the first American war a great demand existed for men, every method and artifice being resorted to in order to enlist or or entrap the unwary. It was no uncommon trick with recruiting parties to present the country lads with lozenges or other confec-

tions with a shilling secreted among them,
which upon the unsuspecting greenhorn taking
in his hand, he was immediately enlisted—and
no entreaties could induce the soldiery to take
back the obnoxious shilling. At other times
they would clandestinely slip a shilling into the
pockets of the unwary, and then claim them
as recruits. Many a hardy and brave mountaineer was thus ensnared, and sent abroad to
fight in defence of his country and native wilds.
One of those who had been thus practised upon
was a young man from the braes of Glen-
Urquhart, who, not relishing the idea of crossing the Atlantic, showed some resistance, in
which he was aided by a few friends, but the
red-coats were too many for them, and for
better security lodged his prize in jail. Upon
this two or three of the captive's female friends
immediately repaired to Sheriff Campbell's
house (now known as Ness House), and requested an interview. The worthy Sheriff,
though entertaining a large party to dinner, immediately came out, and hearing the suit the
females proffered, he instantly proceeded bare-
headed to the jail, and demanded the young
man's immediate liberation, which to the joy of
his friends was quickly granted.

Sheriff Campbell was succeeded by Mr
Fraser of Farraline who likewise was a just
and upright judge, but it can hardly be said
that his decisions were seasoned with that for-

bearance and leniency which distinguished the
trials and judgments of his predecessor. In his
time the French war broke out, and enlistments
were made in a manner equally crafty as in the
days of Sheriff Campbell.   A young man from
Stratherrick who happened to be in Inverness
on a market-day was entrapped by the red-
coats as the Glen-Urquhart lad had been, and
made an appeal to Sheriff Fraser ; but the only
consolation he got was that he could obtain no
redress, for " King George must have men,
come what will, or by whatever manner ; otherwise the French will come over and kill us all."
The poor fellow departed much cast down, followed by a *posse* of red coats.   A countryman,
however, found opportunity to whisper in his
ear to go to the ever ready friend of the poor
and distressed—Mr Macdonell, solicitor.   To
him he accordingly went and mentioned what
the Sheriff had said to him.   On this Mr Macdonell desired him to go immediately back to
the Sheriff, and getting as near as possible to
his person, slip a shilling into his breeches'
pocket, which if he succeeded in doing, he
could claim the Sheriff as his recruit, at the
same time using his own words, namely, "King
George must have men, come what will."
    The Highlander did as desired, and claimed
the worthy administrator of the law as his
lawful recruit, who, in a great rage, said,
"Away home you scoundrel, out of my sight !

I know it was that devil Sandy Macdonell that put you up to this." The now overjoyed Highlander returned to his native hills.

A HIGHLAND DESPERADO.

In byegone times the Highlands were celebrated for giving birth to many strong, robust, and healthy men, some of whom were endowed with more than an ordinary portion of physical powers. Crunar Fraser, the subject of the present tale, was born at Kingellie, in the parish of Kirkhill about the year 1625. As he was rising towards manhood his strength proportionally increased ; but in his disposition he possessed nothing of the meek or amiable, but, on the contrary, was overbearing, unbending, and cruel to excess—so much so that ultimately he was the terror of the country. A new field, however, was opened for him more congenial to his tastes. Through the interest of his chief a commission in the army was procured for him. At this time a civil war broke out in Ireland, and thither Crunar Fraser and his company were ordered ; but as he was leaving his native place his stepmother gave him a Scotch " convoy " the length of Inverness— no doubt inwardly rejoicing at getting off such a ferocious character. On coming to the centre of the bridge, she told him she intended going no farther ; but ere bidding him farewell put a charm around him, which she said would make him invulnerable to either steel or bullet. " And how long is the charm to last ? " asked Crunar. " Until you see my face again," re plied the pretended enchantress, turning away. Crunar's evil genius was in the ascendant, and quick as thought he unsheathed his broadsword, and with one blow severed her head from her body, in the belief that by this barbarous deed the charm would remain with him all his days.

Having joined his regiment in Ireland, he was not long there when his prowess and dar- ing were unequalled, and his hairbreadth escapes were the surprise of the whole army, while his powers as an officer were mercilessly exercised towards all whom the fortunes of war placed within his grasp. To none who fell into his hands was quarter given, but all were cruelly butchered—not even the tender sex being spared. In one instance the agonising en- treaties of a beautiful young lady arrested for a moment his murderous arm as he was in the act of thrusting his sword through the heart of her husband—a gallant and brave officer—but the emotion was merely transitory, for in an in- stant he sacrificed his victim. The lady, to whom he had taken a fancy, was spared with the purpose of carrying her to the Highlands as his bride. Returning from the field, with the lady seated behind him on horseback, and whilst in the act of crossing a bridge, he felt the hands of his fair captive as if searching for something about his person—-probably his dirk or *skiandhu*—he instantly turned round and despatched her, throwing her lifeless body into the rapid stream beneath.

Crunar's warlike exploits and fame in Ireland were greatly lauded by not a few of the clan who remained at home; while there were others who dreaded the worst on his return, but these were agreeably disappointed, he having settled down amongst them as a quiet peaceable farmer, and not the ferocious and bloody soldier they had expected to find him. Some time before his death a company of Irish soldiers was stationed in Inverness, and, learning that Crunar still lived, and that within seven miles of the town, they formed the resolution of going to Kingellie and putting a period to his existence in revenge for the havoc he committed among their countrymen when in Ireland. Crunar, however, was apprised of their intention and approach, and requested those around him to carry him out to the east end of the house. This being done, when the red-coats were about a quarter of a mile off, he raised himself on his elbow, and gave such a tremendous roar as re-echoed amongst the neighbouring hills. The soldiers alarmingly exclaimed that the old fox was powerful as ever, and hastily retraced their steps back to Inverness. Crunar Fraser was never after interfered with, and died in peace at a good old age. His house was ever afterwards haunted ; and honest James Young the weaver,

who was an occupant, according to the legend,
was often tormented with his apparition moving
through the house. At length James became
so well acquainted with the spectre that his
nocturnal visits gave him no uneasiness. The
house has long since crumbled into ruins, not a
vestige of it being visible.

THE BLACKSMITH AND THE LAIRD OF GLENGARRY.

A worthy representative of Vulcan, who resided at the village of Fort-Augustus, had a
pretty large account against the laird of Glengarry for work done, furnished, and delivered ;
but notwithstanding his having called oft and
divers times for payment, he could never obtain
an interview with the debtor chief. His
patience being quite exhausted with dunning,
he on one occasion determined, come what
would, to have a personal conference with the
laird, and, accordingly, with that firm resolve
strengthened at every step, he set out for Inver-
garry House. On arriving, he immediately inquired for the laird. The servant gave the
usual answer—" Yes, but cannot be seen at
present, as he is engaged." The answer was
decisve, and enraged the blacksmith a good
deal, who, without further ceremony, dashed
past the attendant and entered abruptly the
room in which Glengarry was engaged at the

time in conversation with Mr Robert Anderson, the principal innkeeper then in Inverness. They had been transacting some piece of business together, and the unlooked for appearance of the blacksmith, with his black face neither shaven nor shorn, and an apron which seemed from its hue to have been recently used in scouring the anvil, silenced the worthy pair.

But Glengarry, recovering his self-possession, demanded of the intruder what he wanted. "What do I want? Is that ye're saying, laird, then me wants payment o' ma monie." Glengarry, not being in a mood to meet the demand, and fond of a bit of mischief, laid hold of a whip which was at hand, saying—"I'll pay you, you rascal." The blacksmith, aware of the customer he had to deal with, took fright and ran away as fast as he could, pursued by the the laird and Mr Anderson. Having got outside, he tied his apron round his middle, and in right earnest took to his heels. After running some distance, Glengarry gave up the pursuit, leaving it to Mr Anderson to continue the chase, which he did, and after a pretty long run succeeded in laying hold of the poor smith, whom he held until Glengarry came up, when the enraged chieftain bestowed a heavy flogging on his unfortunate creditor.

The latter returned to his house quite a disconsolate man, laughed at by his neighbours, and made the jest of those who patronised his smithy. However, there happened one day

soon thereafter to enter his workshop an itine-
rating skin merchant from Inverness, to whom
he told the whole affair. This sympathising
individual advised him to lose no time in sum-
moning Glengarry and Anderson to appear
before Sheriff Campbell at Inverness. This he
did, and the parties attended, the former at
considerable inconvenience.

The Sheriff, on hearing the case, addressed
Glengarry as follows :—" This is a new way,
laird, of paying old debts, but such conduct
will not and cannot be tolerated, for the time
is now gone bye in which a chieftain or a
laird would use his vassal as a slave. You
are, therefore, to pay the poor man's account
before you move out of the box in which you
sit ; and for beating him with the whip, you
are to give him the fine of fifty pounds Scots."
On Mr Anderson he bestowed a severe repri-
mand for the part he had acted in the business.

Glengarry, to his credit, cheerfully paid
both the account and the fine, and went home
highly pleased with the " pluck" the smith had
shown in bringing him before Sheriff Campbell.

THE REV. MURDO MACKENZIE.[*]

The above clergyman was a member of the
family of Gairloch, and his first outset as a

---

[*] Descended from a common progenitor of the family of
the Mackenzies of Dailuaine, Strathspey.—See Mackenzies
" History and Genealogies of the Mackenzies," 2nd edition,
page 474.

preacher was on being appointed chaplain to a regiment in the army of Gustavus Adolphus, King of Sweden; after which he was settled minister of the parish of Contin, Ross-shire; and from thence translated to Inverness in 1640, where his ministrations were highly appreciated. The "speaking on the question," or the meeting of the "Men," on Fridays before the celebration of the Lord's Supper, originated with Mr Mackenzie—not in the church, however, but in his own house at Kingsmills, in which place, during his incumbency in Inverness, pious laymen were wont to assemble, edifying and instructing each other by stating their own Christian experience, as also their opinions of select passages of the Scriptures. Subsequently the meeting of the "Men" became general throughout the Church in the North. Although Mr Mackenzie had thus begun and established soul-edifying exercises in Inverness, yet he was so disgusted with the impiety of some of his parishioners that he determined on the first opportunity that presented itself to leave the parish. The following ludicrous affair heightened his resolution :—

Whilst addressing the Gaelic congregation from the important words, " Take up thy cross and follow me," a drouthy knight of the awl sat in the gallery in a state of inobriety, listening as attentively as he could to the impressive discourse of the preacher; and the words of the text attracting his attention, it occurred to him to turn them to a subject quite foreign to the purpose. Accordingly, as Mr Mackenzie was returning home in the afternoon, and when ascending the Flesh Market Brae, he was suddenly alarmed by hearing moans and groans immediately behind him. Turning quickly round to his dismay he saw a man carrying a stout woman on his back. The bearer of the unwilling burden was the shoemaker, who, on Mr Mackenzie's demanding to know why he behaved in such a manner to a female, was answered that he was hearing him that day in the Hielan' Kirk, and that he (Mr Mackenzie) desired him to take up his cross and follow him, which he was just doing. The shoemaker had thus persisted in following the worthy minister, and it was only when the latter gave him a sixpence that he could get rid of him, desiring him at the same time to get out of his sight with his abominable cross.

Soon after this unhallowed affair, Mr Mackenzie, in 1645, was translated to Elgin, and on the restoration of Charles II., was consecrated Bishop of the diocese of Moray, on the 1st of May 1662 ; and in the end of the year 1676 was translated to the see of Orkney, where he died in February 1688.

THE REV. JOHN PORTEOUS.

This eminent divine was born in Inverness in the year 1704, and was presented to the united parishes of Daviot and Dunlichity about the latter end of the year 1730. The first place he preached at was Daviot, and although no obstruction was offered by those of that district of the parish, yet he was but coldly received. Next Sabbath-day, when he was to preach at Dunlichity, just as he was entering the church he was not a little surprised to be assailed with a shower of stones, and to his astonishment, he perceived upwards of fifty females, headed by a virago named Elspet Maclean, coming towards him with their aprons tied round their waists, in which were deposited a goodly supply of the article which slew Goliath.

Such unexpected treatment caused Mr Porteous to stand for a moment in suspense; but seeing the women approaching close to him shaking their hands, and also hearing their generalissimo Elspet vociferating, " Let us kill the Whig rascal," at the same time issuing orders to her followers, he judged it the safest course to take to his heels. He ran down the strath towards Daviot, with Elspet and her lawless force in full chase after him, every now and then exclaiming, as she discharged a stone, " Another throw at the Whig minister." Fortunately for him, he could lay no claim to what is alleged of some of our London aldermen—he being a tall but slender person, which no doubt enabled him to outrun his pursuers, particularly for the first three

miles, that is, to Tordarroch ; at which place, on
a little knoll, the curate of the district was holding forth to a large assemblage, and, as ill-luck
would have it, Mr Porteous in his flight had to
pass hard by this congregation, from whom a
large and formidable accession, headed by Rory
Macraibart the tailor, joined Elspet's corps, but
much to the credit of the curate he vehemently
denounced their proceedings.   The reverend
fugitive had now to redouble his exertions to
escape with his life, and the chase was continued
regardless of running streams, which presented
no impediment to Elspet and the tailor's fairy
bands, until they came near Daviot.   It is not
a little remarkable that, although the stones
were flying like hail around him, only two or
three of the enemy's *balls* struck him, the effects
of which were no way serious.

His pursuers having desisted from following
him further, he sat down at the roadside to
draw breath, and no doubt to return grateful
thanks to Providence for the wonderful and
hairbreadth escapes he had made that day—a
day never to be effaced from his mind.   While
he was thus musing, a pious venerable man
came up who sympathised with him very much.
In the course of their conversation, Mr Porteous
said, " Well, well, one thing I will say, that
seven generations shall pass away before the
people of Daviot and Dunlichity will have a
minister who will please them."   This predic-
tion was fulfilled to the very letter.

About the year 1732, and after Mr Porteous had remained upwards of a year in his father's house, he got a presentation to the parish of Kilmuir-Easter, in the Presbytery of Tain, where he met with a far different flock to that of Daviot and Dunlichity, and where he was the honoured instrument of much good. By his sound reasoning and advice he tended greatly to suppress the spirit of rebellion in 1745-46, and along with Lord President Forbes he was constantly urging upon the young Earl of Cromartie to take no part in it. Lord Lovat hearing of Mr Porteous's influence in Easter-Ross, and suspecting the cause of the Earl's backwardness in embracing the Pretender's cause, was constantly despatching his confidential valet, Donald Cameron, with letters to him requesting him not to listen to any suggestions, but to stand firm, as he (Lord Lovat) was to get a dukedom, and was perfectly satisfied that the same title would be conferred on him also. Mr Porteous never married, and it was supposed the cause lay in the conduct of the fair sex at Dunlichity He lived to a good old age, and died greatly lamented by all who knew him. He was cousin to the notorious Captain Porteous whom the mob in Edinburgh hanged in the Grassmarket.

MACKENZIE, 119 126 127 130 131 147 151 157 Alexander 119 Collector 132 George 103 104 105 106 107 108 John 60 61 133 Kenneth 120 121 131 132 Maj 134 Mary 133 Molly 133 Mr 158 183 184 Murdo 44 182 Murdoch 44 Rev 44

MACKINNON, Rory 163

MACKINTOSH, 1 2 3 4 5 27 30 32 35 43 44 47 48 51 82 119 Aeneas 79 Alexander 39 41 46 50 Alister 46 50 52 Angus 6 23 72 Brigadier 29 33 Edward 33 36 39 40 41 Gen 29 Lachlan 2 28 Laird Of 82 Mrs 9 Ned 36 37 Of Borlum 22 Of Lachlan 28 Saunders 50 Shaw 6 William 2 4 23 28 47

MACLEAN, 26 27 29 Elspet 185 Finlay 21 Mr 22 Of Dochgarroch 25 Provost 167 168 169

MACLEOD, Laird Of 92

MACOURLIC, 153 155

MACPHERSON, 28 29 34 35 James 53

MACQUAIN, Rory 173 174

MACRAIBART, Rory 186

MARY, Queen 7

MENZIES, Jean 33

MORAY, 8 Earl Of 8

MUCKLE, Madge 172 Willie The Dyster 47

MUNRO, George 139 Robert 56

NICHOLSON, Mr 65 66 Patrick 59 60 Rev 67

NICOLSON, Malcolm 65 Patrick 65

OSSIAN, 53 122

PATERSON, 135 136

PORTEOUS, Capt 187 John 184 Mr 185 186 187 Rev 94

QUEENSBERRY, 59 Duke Of 58

REDCASTLE, 124 126 Laird Of 121 122 123 131

ROB, Roy 7 37 160

ROBERTSON, Provost 48

RODGER, Rob 64

ROSE, Capt 60

SALTOUN, Lady 4 5 7

SHAW, 33

SHIRRA, Dubh 158 159 160

STAFFORD, Lord 73

STEWART, Thomas 98

STUART, 29 61 63 76 Charles 88 Charles Edward 96

SUTER, James 9

THOMSON, 67 Robert 67

TOLQUHOUN, Laird Of 78

URQUHART, 164 Mrs 102

WALKER, Fountaine 4

WALPOLE, Horace 64

WARRAND, A J 64

WELSH, Mr 127

WILLIAM, Bailies 6 Iii 46 Of Borlum 4 7

YOUNG, James 179

191

www.ingramcontent.com/pod-product-compliance
Lightning Source LLC
Chambersburg PA
CBHW070914270326
41927CB00011B/2570